"A wealth of information . . . a plethora of practical tools . . . a user-friendly reference guide we will return to often. . . . By turning to this delightful book, we learn how to . . . celebrate in a deeper way, build our faith, and grow in understanding of God, ourselves, and those we love."

—*Julie Morris, inspirational speaker and author of 12 books, including* Guided by Him

"As a university professor of parenting and family decisions, I support books that remind parents how tradition and celebrations build stronger family bonds. Poinsett's book does that. It's an easy read, practical, with imaginative, budget-conscious ideas any parent can implement. It doesn't require focused attention nor big slots of time to read. It is a read-me-when-you-need-me book of information and creative ideas for inserting the 'holy' into any holiday."

—*Brenda Nixon, MA, Parenting Author/Educator;* BrendaNixononparenting.blogspot.com

"This book is a wonderful holiday resource—and fun too! Brenda presents useful holiday suggestions with great insight and creativity. This is not only a thoughtful book for parents wanting to build meaningful holidays for their children, but it would also be useful for grandparents, Sunday School teachers, teachers of English-as-a-second-language students, and others wanting to share their Christian heritage with family, friends, and neighbors."

—*Lorraine Powers, Blue River-Kansas City associational WMU adult consultant, Missouri WMU adult special worker, and WMU ambassador*

More New Hope books by

Brenda Poinsett

Can Martha Have a Mary Christmas?
Untangling Expectations and
Truly Experiencing Jesus

The Friendship Factor:
Why Women Need Other Women

Wonder Women of the Bible:
Heroes of Yesterday Who Inspire Us Today

Unwrapping Martha's Joy
Creating a Mary Christmas in Your Heart and Home

Holiday Living

USING YEAR-ROUND HOLIDAYS
TO BUILD FAITH AND FAMILY

Brenda Poinsett

NEW HOPE
PUBLISHERS
Gospel-Centered. Missions-Driven.

BIRMINGHAM, ALABAMA

New Hope® Publishers
P. O. Box 12065
Birmingham, AL 35202-2065
NewHopeDigital.com
New Hope Publishers is a division of WMU®.

Library of Congress Cataloging-in-Publication Data
Poinsett, Brenda.
  Holiday living : using year-round celebrations to build faith and family / Brenda Poinsett.
    p. cm.
  ISBN 978-1-59669-359-3 (pbk.)
1. Holidays--Religious aspects--Christianity. 2. Holidays--United States--Planning. 3. Families--Religious life. I. Title.
  BV30.P65 2013
  263--dc23
                    2012034898

Cover and Interior Design: Glynese Northam

ISBN-10: 1-59669-359-2
ISBN: 978-1-59669-359-3

N134102 • 0113 • 3M1

Dedicated to

Aili,
Noah, and
Christophe

Contents

Acknowledgments

In this book I mention "celebration circle" numerous times, referring to those times when we celebrate around the dining table or seated in a circle in the living room. These are treasured moments. Writing a book takes a circle too—a circle of people who believe in the project and want to help. Below are people who made up the writing circle for this book. Some helped with research, many helped with prayers, others shared ideas, and some helped with housework! All are treasured, and I'm very appreciative. I work better when surrounded by a circle.

Bob Poinsett
Ben Poinsett
Janice Sitzes
Judy Mills
Jan Turner
Scott Andresen
Julie Andresen
Donna Coleman
Jim Tayon
Rhonda Myers
Don Huber
Annette Huber
Ruth Scott
Jane Barton

Barbara Williams
Chris Dulworth
Margie Cruse
Janet Smith
Amy Gaugh
Scenic Regional librarians
Joyce Dinkins
Andrea Mullins
Kathryne Solomon
Tina Atchenson
Sue Badeau
Sue Johnson

Holidays, Holy Days

*E*ureka! A teachable moment! Perhaps a spiritual one! Certainly a *family one!* These thoughts swirled around in my head because I was excited. I had noticed a potential learning atmosphere around our house as Christmas approached, probably because I was a schoolteacher before I became a mother. As a teacher, I wouldn't have dared to hang so many decorations if there wasn't going to be a corresponding lesson!

My husband, Bob, and I capitalized on this environment by using holidays—first Christmas and then branching out to other holidays— to turn our family's attention to God. This way the holidays became vehicles for instruction and worship just as the Feast of Unleavened Bread, the Feast of Weeks, and the Feast of Ingathering were for God's Chosen People. Our holidays became special, set-apart days. They became *holy days*. Would something like this interest you?

Not if it's holy!

Some people back off from anything described as *holy*. If a day were holy, it would be plain, empty, stern, dull, and certainly no fun! But holidays that are holy days can be meaningful, cheerful, interesting, and enjoyable. Here's how.

Know your holiday. With holidays, it is easy to focus more on the means of celebrating rather than the reason. The significance of the day—why it became a holiday in the first place—may have gotten lost through the years. The way we celebrate may become the focus rather than the meaning. For example, as a child, I knew St. Patrick's

11

Day as a day to avoid getting pinched by wearing green and to make shamrocks out of green construction paper. For my children I wanted something more so I investigated. I learned St. Patrick was a missionary to Ireland. He had won hundreds to Christ. Sharing his story with our children turned March 17 into a holy day.

Showcase your faith. Not all of the holidays we observe have a spiritual origin as St. Patrick's does, but usually there's some significant reason for the holiday's existence. This reason is often noble or at least it is something worthy of society's remembering, so the day has potential for connecting it with our faith. Labor Day is an example. This holiday is an opportunity for us to highlight the value of work—something the Bible has much to say about.

Honor God. Learning undergirds, strengthens, and motivates worship. It raises awareness, helps us to focus, increases our appreciation, and gives us a vocabulary to express ourselves—all important aspects of worship. In making the most of the learning environment that prevails at holidays, they can become occasions for honoring God. We can attribute worth to Him, to what He does, and to who He is. We may do this directly by speaking to Him through prayer, praise, and singing, or we can talk about Him to others by extolling His virtues or reminding each other about what God deems important. If we want our children to "serve him," then let them "hear from us about the wonders of the Lord" (Psalm 22:30 TLB).

Think circle. Right off, in raising children, I realized how separated the spiritual aspects of our lives were. We parted ways at the church house door. Adults did things with adults, and children did things with children. I longed to do something spiritual with my children, something the whole family was involved in. When we started learning, sharing, and worshipping together at holiday time, this became possible if I kept the circle concept in mind. It was my working image for bringing us together whether it was sitting in a circle in the family room, seated around our rectangular dining room table, or going as a unit to sing carols at a nursing home. During these circle times, our family life was enriched as we had face-to-face conversations, interacted with each other, and focused on God. At times, we widened our circle and invited others to celebrate with us. I'm a grandmother now, and I still want to experience circle togetherness.

Plan for enjoyment. Bob and I never wanted to take away the feel of the holiday when we learned and worshipped together. We wanted to still have some fun, and fun can actually be beneficial for making holidays holy days. Fun can set the stage for learning and create emotional warmth that contributes to shared worship experience and family togetherness. On occasions, some solemnity is appropriate and effective such as an austere meal the night before the big Thanksgiving feast to encourage feelings of gratitude or a solemn candlelight service on Good Friday to appreciate Christ's suffering. By and large, though, putting the holy into a holiday means enjoyable times.

Some of the activities a family does together may be so well liked that they become family traditions. They will be things children will look forward to year after year and give them a sense of identity. You'll know this is happening if you hear your child bragging to another child about what your family does together. Last December, as a playmate of our grandson's walked by a Christmas wall hanging with emblems about Jesus, he asked, "What's this?" Christophe explained that it was an activity we do each year to celebrate Jesus. With pride he said, "This is something we *always* do."

Do you want to do things with your children or grandchildren that celebrate and recognize your faith? Do you have things you want them to know? Do you want them to grasp your faith? Do you want them to have a sense of a godly heritage? Are there truths you want them to hold on to and remember? Do you want to have enjoyable times together as a family?

Most parents and grandparents want their children and grandchildren to learn about God and their Christian heritage and values, but may be stymied about how to go about it. Just how do you put the holy into holidays?

The question of how

In that first Christmas when I had the "eureka" moment, it was easy. A friend gave us a punch out cardboard Nativity scene. Once we punched out the characters, then it was important to know who they were and what they did, so we turned to the Bible, learned together, and turned our focus to God. Other ideas followed which for Christmas was easy enough because it is a celebration of Jesus' birth, and it is celebrated in a variety of ways—ways we could connect with our faith. But when we started aiming to make other holidays holy, we were challenged. Ideas didn't come as readily. Some ideas we were able to reuse for several years, but children grow and change. Family dynamics change too. This called for fresh ideas. Some of the things we did for several years, but eventually we outgrew them. And some ideas we tried were only worthy of one year's observance; obviously they were never meant to become traditions!

While I was sold on putting the holy into holidays, coming up with ways to do this kept me searching. Maybe I worked extra hard at this because I was selective. I wanted ideas that didn't require a great deal of preparation and were easy to implement. Is there ever enough time to do all the things you want to do or need to do around a holiday? Certainly, at Christmas this is true, but even other holidays can catch busy adults by surprise. *Oh my, tomorrow is Veterans Day, and I haven't even given it a thought.*

I wanted the idea to be workable. As an educator, I was used to theories, and to my chagrin, I had learned some theories don't always work in the classroom where you are interacting with live, thinking individuals! When I considered ideas, I asked myself, *Would this idea be something that our family would respond to? Would it easily merge in with the flow of our family life?*

I wanted the idea to be effective. Would it draw our attention to God? Would it provide us an opportunity to talk with God or to talk about Him? Would it emphasize something about our faith?

Not only did I want the ideas to be easy to implement, workable, and effective, I wanted them to be inexpensive because our family always seemed to be living on a limited budget. Fortunately, holy, I learned, doesn't cost a lot of money!

Finding ideas that met my criteria was challenging. Many times I longed for a resource book that I could go to where easy-to-implement, workable, effective, inexpensive, enjoyable ideas would be available. I never found that resource, but keeping the holy into holidays was so important to Bob and me that I kept looking. I saved and collected the ideas I found. I shared those ideas with other parents and grandparents in celebration workshops, and they shared their ideas with me. Now after collecting for many years, I'm sharing them in this book. The resource I couldn't find is now available for you.

If putting the holy into holidays is something you want to experience with your family, here's the place to look. This book is chock-full of ideas for learning, worshipping, and celebrating together as a family.

What you'll find

Each chapter will be devoted to a particular holiday. Most chapters will include some background information about the holiday, particularly how it got started and why it is significant. What you read will sharpen your awareness, remind you of what is important, and help you think about what you might want to emphasize in your holiday observance. If you want to know more, research the holiday at your local library or on the Internet. Looking for more information could in and of itself be an activity for you and your family members to do together. Nevertheless, the information in this book will be enough to get you launched.

Along with the background information, you will find suggestions for connecting with your faith and honoring God. With some holidays like Christmas or Easter, this will be easy enough, but other days may call for a little more thought, particularly the secular holidays. Some secular days (days without a religious origin) are included in this book, and here's why. The holidays chosen for this book are ones that many of us peg our lives around. In other words, they're the ones your kids come home from school talking about, showing you related crafts they've made or pictures they have drawn. These days are also ones emphasized or highlighted in the news or in your grocery store ads. These are the days on which some people don't have to go to work. Consequently, these days are in our thoughts and in our consciousness, providing an environment ripe for learning and worshipping.

Regardless of whether the day highlighted in each chapter is religious or secular—or a mix!—the book's emphases will be on centering your family's attention on your faith. In this way, all the holidays have potential for becoming holy days. This doesn't mean your family needs to observe all of them. We don't. We choose those holidays that we want to celebrate and that emphasize what we want to emphasize. In the same way, you might want to pick and choose the days that your family wants to acknowledge. While remembering the Sabbath day to keep it holy is a commandment, there is not one that says, "Make all holidays holy." You may feel free to be selective in what you choose to do. What suits your family? What pricks your interest? What meets your goals? What days best accentuate your faith?

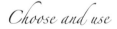

Choose and use

The ideas for putting the holy into the holidays you select to celebrate will be easy-to-implement, workable, effective, and inexpensive. Several ideas will be presented in each chapter, more in some than in others. You can evaluate the ideas and select the one or two ideas that are just right for your family. How big your family is, the ages of your children, their willingness or unwillingness to cooperate, the space in your home, your particular tastes, and the amount of time you have will affect your decision. In your home, you may have one parent or two, children or no children, all adults or mostly children, one generation or three as is currently in ours. Whatever your situation, there are ideas you can use in this book.

As you read these ideas, you'll see that putting the holy into holidays doesn't have to be elaborate or complicated; neither does it have to be simple, although I'm partial to simple. Simple is more easy to manage, something important to time-pressed adults. Besides, I believe God is more apt to respond to us in simplicity, or maybe it is that we are more apt to be listening and looking for Him! When our celebrations are simple, when we are not distracted by elaborate preparations or overindulging ourselves, we can experience God as well as honor Him. He responds to us and blesses us, and that just may be the best part of putting the holy into holidays. God gives back, and we experience Him together as a family. This is something worth pursuing!

Putting the holy into holidays at home is doing something out of the ordinary, something you don't do every day, and doing something that honors God or recognizes our faith. There are numerous ways of doing this as this book will reveal. Some may not fit your situation but many will! You'll find ideas just right for your group—for when it is just your family or when you want to reach out to include others— ideas that will give you meaningful and joyful holidays. It's a joy to know we please God by honoring Him, to know we invest in our children's spiritual growth, to experience good times with them, and to be blessed by God in return. All of this can be ours when we put the holy into holidays. As you discover this, you, too, may want to shout "Eureka!" as you realize you have discovered ways to have teachable, memorable, spiritual moments with your family.

New Year's

"Forgetting those things which are behind, and reaching
forth unto those things which are before"
(Philippians 3:13 KJV).

Sometime during the year, all over the world, people say good-bye to the old year and welcome a new one. Celebrating the new year is something people have been doing for a long, long time, even before people had calendars. Certain events made them think that an old year had passed and a new one had begun. For some, it was the warming of the earth each spring. For others, a new year began with a harvest. Eventually, with the development of a widely accepted calendar, January 1 marked the beginning of a new year for much of the world.[1]

As one year ends and another begins, people celebrate with noise, hilarity, parties, food, parades, and football. However you choose to celebrate, you can also honor God and emphasize your faith. This could be at a special New Year's Eve meal when you are all seated around the table, late on New Year's Eve during that last hour before the clock strikes midnight, or on New Year's Day morning with a leisurely brunch after everyone has slept in. This set-apart time will provide an opportunity to look back and to look ahead.

Looking back

To look back doesn't mean the past year has to be thoroughly analyzed or every aspect covered. Who you are celebrating with—

small children, teens, adults or all ages—might determine what you choose to review. What kind of year you had might also figure in to this exercise! The point of looking back is to realize how God blessed you, how He helped you persevere, how He helped you navigate changes, or what He taught you. Here are some ways to do this.

Gather items that represent important happenings of your family in the last year. Display these items on a tray. Give each person a pencil and paper, and then bring out the tray. Walk slowly by participants, letting them get a good look, and then take the tray out of sight. Ask them to write down what items they remember and what they stand for. When it appears the group can recall no more, bring the tray back in, and discuss the items one by one.

Consider creations. Ask family members to share their most significant writing, art, or photography from the past year. This could range anywhere from a six-year-old's artwork to an unusual picture captured on a phone. Ask them to bring their creations to the dining table to share when you partake of a memorable meal of traditional foods—things your family always eats on New Year's. Being close together at the table will facilitate looking at each other's work.

Recall significant events. Page Hughes in *Party with a Purpose* suggests dividing your celebration group into two teams. She says, "Have them list the most significant events of the last year. The team that comes up with the most events wins."[2] The significant events could be those of your family, your church, your community, or the nation. The choice is yours! The prize could be noisemakers. After a review of significant events, you'll be ready to celebrate when the clock strikes midnight.

Organize a talent night for New Year's Eve. Each person must prepare a performance of some kind for the rest to enjoy. No one is excluded! It could be a new song learned, a poem they found and liked, a magic trick, a horn solo, playing "Twinkle, Twinkle, Little Star" on the piano, or juggling three balls in the air. Everyone has learned or experienced something in the past year so make New

Year's Eve a festive time of sharing. As you see and hear each other's talents, your appreciation for one another will increase. It will also reinforce the biblical truth that we all have something to give.

Measure your growth. With your fellow celebrants sitting in a circle, ask, How much have you grown in the last year? Have a yardstick in hand. Pass the yardstick around the circle. Ask each person to show on the stick how much he or she has grown in the last year. Little children might want to talk about how tall they are now compared to last year. For others, the growth could be in knowledge, skills, or attitudes. In some way or other, we all grew in some way in the last year. Even an inch's growth calls for celebration. We made progress! Conclude this activity by mentioning the Golden Rule (Luke 6:31), something we all want to keep in mind as we enter a new year.

Encourage testimonies. If your celebration circle is small, invite everyone to answer a question similar to one of these: What has God done in your life in the past year? What evidence have you seen of God's handiwork? What Bible verse has meant the most to you? If you are celebrating with a large group, invite two or three people who have had a challenging or victorious last year to share their testimonies.

Follow any of these looking-back activities by saying, "Aren't we blessed? Let's thank God for this past year." With awareness raised, thanksgiving should flow.

Recalling in some way the past year can be insightful and can lead to being more grateful or more observant about what God is doing, but New Year's is also about the future. Here's where the *New* in *New* Year needs to be emphasized. As the Apostle Paul recommended, we want to reach "forth unto those things which are before" (Philippians 3:13 KJV).

Thinking ahead

Just saying "*new* year" implies an opportunity to start over, to begin again, to have another chance. There's a new year ahead with 365 new days! With calendars, journals, and scrapbooks, stir up mental juices, think about various possibilities, build dreams, and open yourselves up for God to bless you.

Provide calendars for family members. Sit around the table together and write the names of family members and friends on their birthdays. Note special events you want to participate in. For young children, have stickers available to put on special days. Talk about other things you might like to add such as a summer missions trip or a fall retreat. Print a Bible verse on the calendar's cover—one you want to claim for the coming year.

Give each family member a brand-new journal for a brand-new year. Together have everyone make the first entry either by answering a question or completing a statement.

- What do I want to see happen in the coming year?
- What do I hope will happen?
- What do I want God to do with my life in the coming year?
- "I look forward to . . ."
- "I'm hoping this year will be the year I . . ."
- "My prayer for this year is . . ."

While this may sound like it is an adult-only activity, young children can and do write in journals. Some schools in my area have them doing this as early as kindergarten. Journal writing doesn't have to be perfect; it just needs to be genuine. However, if journal writing is too intimidating for your family, encourage them to make "dream books" instead.

Give family members inexpensive scrapbooks, old magazines, scissors, and glue. Ask them to look through magazines for pictures of what they would like to see happen or what they would like to accomplish in the coming year. Clip out the pictures and glue them in the scrapbooks, turning it into a dream book. Their mental juices will flow as they look through the magazine and talk with each other as they clip and glue. They'll sense possibilities for the new year and dream dreams.

With a calendar, a journal, or a dream book, you can look at it from time to time during the year to remind you of what you were hoping for at the first of the year and to evaluate how you are doing. Repeating your calendar verse, rereading journal entries or reviewing your dream book keeps alive your hopes and fans your faith.

Pressing toward the mark

Out of the above activities, some resolutions may emerge. Is there anything more associated with New Year's than making resolutions? Making resolutions is a good practice but many people balk at the idea. As one person said, "Making a promise to change in the coming year is a classic invitation to failure." But if we want to make the most of the new year, some resolving is helpful. Here are some ways to encourage resolution keeping.

Sweeten your resolve with a resolution cake. In her book *Saintly Celebrations & Holy Holidays*, Bernadette McCarver Snyder, suggests collecting game pieces such as a thimble, a shoe, a horse, or a car (sounds like these come from Monopoly!) or buying small figures at a hobby shop or toy store. A few days before New Year's, ask each family member to choose the figure that could represent his or her resolution, but not tell what the resolution is. Make your family's favorite cake and decorate the top with the symbols chosen. "Put the cake on a nice platter or tray and surround it with New Year decorations: confetti, streamers, party hats, noise makers. At dessert time, cut the cake and give each person the piece with the symbol he or she has chosen."[3] Encourage each person to share his resolution with the group. "For the rest of the year, whenever you serve cake ask, 'Do you remember our resolution cake? Are you keeping your resolutions?'"[4] According to Snyder, this could lead to groans or giggles. Hopefully, it will lead to success!

Add some accountability. Write out your resolutions, seal them in envelopes, and address them to yourself. Say something like this,

"You are all invited back next New Year's Day for supper. At that time, we'll open our envelopes and see how we did. You might discover that you changed your expectations during the year or you might be able to exclaim, 'I did it!' Either way, we'll be able to celebrate growth." Or you may not want to wait that long. Mail them in six months with a cheerful "How are you doing? I'm praying for you" greeting.

Press on with prayer. We can pray for ourselves as we begin the new year and as we working at keeping resolutions. We can draw names and agree to pray for each other through out the year, revealing next New Year's who we have been praying for. We can pray individually, out loud for each other as a part of our New Year's celebration. Or we can pray a group prayer together. I like this group prayer from the book *The Heavenly Party*: "Lord, the year ahead is an unknown, but we face it with you. Help us to take hold of your hand and to walk into it with trust, confidence and strength, and whatever it may hold, let there be moments of sweetness for each and every one of us."[5]

Make it goals instead of resolutions. A resolution is a promise you make to yourself to change something in your life. A goal, to me, is more positive. It is not something I have to change, but it is something I can move toward. The difference in the two words may be only slight, but it is enough to help me. It's the way "I press toward the mark . . . of the high calling of God in Christ Jesus" (Philippians 3:14 KJV).

The New Year's celebration may be about setting individual goals or group goals. Use a leisurely New Year's brunch or lunch to set goals with others. Here are some examples.

- As a family, let's memorize 52 Bible verses in the coming year (1 a week) or let's take one missions trip together.
- As a couple, let's have a date night once every month in the new year or let's plant a garden together in the spring and raise vegetables.
- As a Sunday School class, let's aim to add five new members this year or let's memorize the books of the Bible.

Follow the setting of goals with supportive, encouraging words and prayers. Rejoice at what you've decided because this means the new year is full of possibilities!

As we look back, as memories are recalled, as we count our blessings and gain a vision for year ahead, we're going to feel like celebrating. That's when it's time to "make a joyful noise unto God" (Psalm 66:1 KJV). Bring out the kazoos, ring the bells, bang on pans, cheer loudly, and sing vibrantly. "This is the [holiday] which the Lord hath made; we will rejoice and be glad in it" (Psalm 118:24 KJV).

CHAPTER 3

Martin Luther King Jr. Day

*"For there is no difference between Jew and Gentile
— the same Lord is Lord of all and richly blesses
all who call on him" (Romans 10:12).*

Every year on the third Monday in January, Americans recognize the birthday of Martin Luther King Jr. He wasn't a President like Abraham Lincoln or an explorer like Columbus who discovered a new land, so why is he honored? Many men have lived great lives and done significant things without having a holiday named after them. Why do we remember Martin Luther King Jr.?

Who was he?

Martin Luther King Jr. was born January 15, 1929, and raised in a Christian home. His parents taught their children to treat all people fairly. Young Martin, though, noticed that all people were not treated fairly. He especially noticed that African Americans were treated differently. African Americans had to use different drinking fountains and different restrooms. They had to sit in the back of buses and let white people have the seats at the front. They had to eat at different restaurants. Black children could not go to school with white children all because of the color of their skin.

In his heart, young Martin knew this kind of treatment was not right. When he grew up and studied to be a minister, his education confirmed his convictions and also expanded his thinking. He realized things didn't have to be the way they were. People's attitudes and behavior could be transformed. Unfair laws could be changed, and they could be changed peacefully. When he became the pastor of Dexter Avenue Baptist Church in Montgomery, Alabama, something happened that made him realize it was time to initiate change.

Rosa Parks, an African American woman who lived in Montgomery, was arrested for refusing to give up her bus seat to a white man. Inspired by her courage, Dr. King asked members of the African American community not to ride buses in Montgomery until segregation laws were lifted. They found other ways to get to where they were going. If they were arrested or mistreated, Dr. King urged them to remain peaceful, and they did.

Their nonviolent resistance worked! After 382 days, African Americans in Montgomery earned the right to sit anywhere they wanted on city buses. They also did not have to give up their seats to white passengers. The Supreme Court made laws requiring segregation on buses unconstitutional.

After this, Dr. King and more than 100 African American leaders formed the Southern Christian Leadership Conference (SCLC). Their purpose was to organize nonviolent protests wherever discrimination was being practiced. This led to extensive travel for Dr. King.

As the SCLC's president, he made speeches and advised people on how to work for change. He staged marches, boycotts, and protests, trying all the while to keep them nonviolent, but he wasn't always successful.

Many people praised Dr. King and followed him, but others didn't like him. When Dr. King went to Memphis, Tennessee, to help sanitation workers in 1968, he was killed by someone who hated him.

His death by violent means made people realize that things must be changed in this country, and they have. Attitudes, behavior, and laws have changed, but there's still work to do. This is one reason why pausing to remember him every January is important. Focusing on his life and work remind us that we are to always to be about bringing people together and treating each other fairly.

To round out this story, to make it fuller and to learn more about this great man, gather your family members around a computer screen or in front of your television. In pictures, in film, and in commentary on the Internet, there's an abundance of information about Martin Luther King Jr. CDs and DVDs are available at your public library. This celebrated person is one you can still see in action and hear him speak. One thing in particular that you will want to listen to is Dr. King's "I have a dream" speech.

I have a dream

Dr. King taught through powerful speeches that even if we look different from one another, we should still respect each other. He and other African American leaders worked hard to change laws and improve lives. Two of those leaders, A. Philip Randolph and Bayard Rustin, planned a march for jobs and freedom in Washington, D. C., in 1963.

The march took place on a hot August day. More than 250,000 people turned out to march orderly and peacefully. Then they listened to speeches. Dr. King was the last speaker of the day. As he stood before the huge crowd, he delivered his written speech. He told them about his hopes for freedom and equality. Then as if moved by God, he put aside his notes and spoke from the heart. He told them about his dream for the future of America—a dream that has been inspiring people ever since.

You can capture some of his speech with this responsive reading. I have taken a few liberties with the text for ease of reading, to include daughters along with sons, and to keep people from having to try to say *prodigious*.

LEADER: "I have a dream that one day this nation will rise up and live out the true meaning of its creed."

ALL: "We hold these truths to be self-evident, that all men and women are created equal."

LEADER: "I have a dream that one day the sons and daughters of former slaves and the sons and daughters of former slave-owners will be able to sit down together at the table of brotherhood and sisterhood."

CHILD 1: "People will be not be judged by the color of their skin, but by the content of their character."

CHILD 2: "Every valley shall be exalted, every hill and mountain shall be made low."

CHILD 3: "The rough places shall be made plain."

CHILD 4: "The crooked places shall be made straight and the glory of the Lord will be revealed and all flesh shall see it together."

LEADER: "This will be the day when all of God's children will be able to sing with new meaning, 'My country, 'tis of thee; sweet land of liberty; of thee I sing, land where my fathers died; land of the pilgrim's pride; from every mountainside, let freedom ring.'"

CHILD 1: "Let freedom ring from the high hills of New Hampshire."

CHILD 2: "Let freedom ring from the mighty mountains of New York."

CHILD 3: "Let freedom ring from Stone Mountain, Georgia."

CHILD 4: "Let freedom ring from every hill and molehill in Mississippi."

ALL: "From every mountainside, let freedom ring."

LEADER: "When we allow freedom to ring from every town and every hamlet, from every state and every city we will be able to speed up that day when all of God's children—black men and women, white men and women, Jews and Gentiles, Catholics and Protestants will be able to join hands and shout together."

ALL: "Free at last! Free at last! Thank God Almighty, we are free at last!"

What's your dream?

Follow your listening or reading of the speech with some around-the-table dream-building exercises for bringing people together.

Ask questions. Depending on who is gathered at the table—and their ages—throw out some of these questions for meaningful conversation.

- *Why is having a dream important? What difference does it make?*
- *What is your dream for your church?*
- *What is your dream for your neighborhood or community?*
- *What is your dream for your nation?*
- *Are these dreams in any way related to Jesus' words in Acts 1:8? Could His words be a dream for us to fulfill?*
- *Why is it important to keep Martin Luther King Jr.'s dream alive?*

Share observations. Young children may not be able to comprehend the idea of a "dream" for their church or community, so ask them if they have noticed anyone being mistreated at school, at the park, or in your neighborhood. Have they noticed anyone being treated unfairly because of the color of their skin, a physical handicap, the way they talk, or their size? Martin Luther King Jr. had eyes to see long before his dream began to take shape. Your children have observant eyes; they just may need a different way to talk about what they see.

Draw pictures. In his "I have a dream" speech, Dr. King described a scene nearly every time he repeated the phrase "I have a dream." Children may draw pictures of what they see happening—perhaps two pictures. One picture would be of mistreatment and the second one would be of correct treatment.

Make a chain. To encourage a dream of unity, have children make a chain of people who are different from each other. Prepare ahead of time numerous flat cutouts of people. Make sure the arms are long so the people can be connected. Cut out the people. Give them to the children and ask them to color them, put faces on them, dress them, etc. You'll want to have crayons, markers, paper or fabric scraps, glue, and assorted decorative items available. The children are specifically not to make everyone look alike. They are all to be different, particularly their skin color. In addition to the people figures, have some colored strips of paper available. Use the strips to assemble the chain of people. Glue each paper person's hands together, and then connect the people with the colored strips. Loop each strip through the connected hands of one paper person with the connected hands of another paper person. Display this paper chain as a reminder of Dr. King's dream of a world where people are united.

Connect and sing. If making people figures sounds too daunting, the same impression could be achieved by making a paper chain. Use strips of red, yellow, black, and white construction paper. Cut them out with the children. Paste the colored strips together, display over a door, on the fireplace mantel, or even around the room if the chain is long enough! Talk about the variety of colors in the chain and sing together this song.

> *Jesus loves the little children,*
> *All the children of the world;*
> *Red and yellow, black and white,*
> *They are precious in His sight,*
> *Jesus loves the little children of the world.*

Connect and pray. Don't know this song about children of the world? Simply repeat the words together as a prayer.

> *Jesus, we thank You that You love little children,*
> *that You love all the children of the world.*
> *Red and yellow, black and white.*
> *They are precious in Your sight.*
> *Thank You for loving the children of the world.*

The power of songs

Martin Luther King Jr. utilized the power of song. The protestors he organized frequently sang as they worked against injustices. He also mentioned songs in speaking and in leading people to make changes. Here are three that he used.

1. "We Shall Overcome." The people sang this at many of their protests, and they sang it as they marched on Washington. Listen to this song on the internet, learn the words, and sing it as a group. Ask your group, what kind of feelings does it stir within? Why do you think it helped people peacefully pursue equality?

2. "America" ("My Country, 'Tis of Thee"). In his "I have a dream" speech, Dr. King called the listeners' attention to the first verse of this song and repeated the last line, "Let freedom ring," again and again. After you have talked about the legacy of Martin Luther King or after you have done the responsive reading above, sing this song. Then at the end, have everyone shout together "Let freedom ring."

3. "Mine Eyes Have Seen the Glory" ("Battle Hymn of the Republic"). In a speech at Memphis, the night before he died, Dr. King mentioned this song. He said: "Like anybody else, I would like to live a long life. . . . But I'm not concerned about that now. I just want to do God's will. And He's allowed me to go up to the mountain and see the Promised Land. And I'm not fearing any man. Mine eyes have seen the glory of the coming of the Lord!"[1]

Celebrate Dr. King's birthday by singing one of these songs. Or you may want to use his example to think of a theme song for your family. What one song states what you believe? What song would hold your family together in challenging times? What hymn or praise chorus strengthens your resolve to pursue a dream? What song best fits your family's wishes for peace?

Pursuing peace peacefully

Three strong influences melded together while Dr. King was studying to be a minister to lead him to believe that change was possible through nonviolent means. If people stood together and refused to obey unjust laws they could peacefully bring about change. Those three influences were Mohandas Gandhi, Henry David Thoreau, and the Bible. What does the Bible say about how we are to view and to treat each other? This holiday can be an incentive for opening your Bible.

- Read, discuss, and memorize some of these Bible verses.

     Genesis 1:27
     Acts 10:34–35
     Galatians 3:28
     James 2:1–4
     1 John 2:9–11

- Read the story of the Samaritan woman at the well in John 4:4–42. The Samaritans hated the Jews and the Jews hated the Samaritans. Ask, How did Jesus view the Samaritans? What do His actions show?

- Read Jesus' story about the Good Samaritan (Luke 10:25–37). Why is the Samaritan the hero in the story? What does the story teach about who is our neighbor?

- Direct your group to the story of Cornelius (a Gentile) and Peter (a Jew) in Acts 10:1–48. Or have children or teens act out the story to see how God through Jesus was bringing about a change in the Jewish-Gentile relationship.

- Read this portion of Jesus' Sermon on the Mount: Matthew 5:38–42. Ask, How could this passage be used to fight for peace when it seems like such a passive concept?

Renewing your commitment to the truths expressed in these scriptures would be an excellent way to honor both Dr. King and God.

Pursuing peace actively

"Faith without deeds is dead" (James 2:26). In other words, if you really believe something you will act on that belief. The conviction Dr. King had about transformation being possible through nonviolent means would have remained dead and laws gone unchanged if he hadn't acted on what he believed. What are some actions we can take on Dr. King's birthday that will pay tribute to him and at the same time promote peace?

- Get to know your neighbors by offering to shovel snow and talking with them. Getting to know people breaks down barriers and promotes understanding which contributes to peace.

- Visit a neighborhood in which you do not live and see if there is some contribution you could make. In 1994, Congress made Martin Luther King Jr. Day a national day of volunteer service.[2] Follow through on what you see with a service project that would improve the quality of life in this neighborhood.

- Invite friends of different cultures and backgrounds to your home for a meal. Ask each one to bring a dish that represents their culture. Yes, you really can feast on sushi and tacos at the same meal! The various dishes served together can be a tangible reminder that we can live together peacefully.

- On the Sunday before the third Monday in January, attend a worship service at a church with a congregation made up largely of people of a race different from your own.

- Attend one of the many memorial services that occur on the third Monday in January. Let your presence say, "I support the dream of Martin Luther King Jr. I work for peace."

- March in a parade. Some communities have parades to honor Dr. King on his birthday. Fall in step with the marchers or organize your own parade. Let the world know you are taking a stand to make it a better place!

Encouraging peace

Dr. King's efforts to combine Christian ideals with nonviolent techniques wasn't easy. He was arrested more than 20 times and assaulted on at least 4 occasions. At times he was discouraged, but he also experienced times of encouragement such as when he was awarded the Nobel Peace Prize. This is a special honor involving a large amount of money, but Dr. King did not keep the prize money. He gave it to other people who were supporting the civil rights movement. Nevertheless, the prize gave him recognition and exposure. It encouraged him to carry on.

- Who is the peace maker in your family? Make a trophy and honor him or her with it at your main meal on Martin Luther King Jr. Day. Give him or her a *Noble* Peace Prize. No monetary reward is necessary, but it can be a time for recognition and encouragement to keep on keeping on.

- Who is a peacemaker in your community? Who is making a difference in troubled areas? Recognize him or her at a community memorial service for Dr. King.

- If there is not community service, write the community peacemaker a letter, thanking him or her for their efforts on behalf of others.

Peacemakers need encouragement, and on this holiday, when we can thank God for the life of Martin Luther King Jr., we can thank a person for continuing to promote peace and understanding.

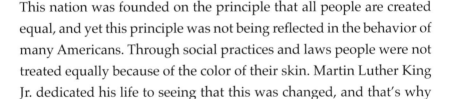

This nation was founded on the principle that all people are created equal, and yet this principle was not being reflected in the behavior of many Americans. Through social practices and laws people were not treated equally because of the color of their skin. Martin Luther King Jr. dedicated his life to seeing that this was changed, and that's why we remember him and celebrate his birthday.

Valentine's Day

"We love him, because he first loved us" (1 John 4:19).

I grimace and I smile when I study Valentine's Day. My forehead wrinkles up as I try to learn the *real* reason for the holiday's beginning. I find various explanations and details that don't agree. This is frustrating. I want to "get it right" so I can share accurate information.

But I also smile as I marvel at how people hold on to celebrating at this time of year even when the reasons and customs change. Even if they don't know for certain the origin of the holiday, they still want to acknowledge it. It is as if a need for a mid-February holiday is built into our DNA. How about you? Do you like something festive to brighten winter's dark days?

If you do, you keep the flavor of this holiday we've come to like and give it a spiritual emphasis. Since it isn't a well-defined holiday, we can define it. I'm going to define it as a holiday about love.

Love and marriage

Various sources trace Valentine's Day to *Lupercalia* [loo-pur-KAY-lee-uh],[1] an ancient Roman festival observed on February 15. Lupercalia was a lover's holiday; some have even called it a fertility festival. It paired members of the opposite sex together, looked forward to the coming of spring, and honored the gods Juno and Pan.

Years later after Roman society became Christianized, the pope made this holiday Christian by naming it after a saint. It became known as Saint Valentine's Day and was celebrated on February 14, the day Saint Valentine was martyred.

While Juno and Pan were no longer honored, the emphasis on the attraction that draws men and women together couldn't be put to rest. People seemed to want—and to need—a celebration of romantic love, and why not? As the Song of Songs illustrates so eloquently, it is a part of God's design for us, built into the way He created us.

At a time when marriages need strengthening, and marriage partners need encouragement, rekindling martial love would be a good holiday emphasis.

Rekindle by repeating. Ask your pastor to schedule a time for renewal of vows maybe at a special Valentine's Day event or on the Sunday nearest Valentine's Day. If the renewal is on Sunday, the pastor could ask couples who want to renew their vows to come to the altar. He could read some simple vows, ask the couples to repeat the vows to each other, and then pray for them.

Rekindle through looking at your wedding photos or of pictures taken of you since your marriage. Spend the evening of Valentine's Day together sorting pictures and possibly making a small scrapbook of selected pictures.

Rekindle through remembering. Play "remember when" as in remember when you first met, when you had your first date, when you fell in love, when you decided to marry, when you bought your home or rented your first place, or when you brought your first child home from the hospital. This activity will unite you together in a desire to carry on.

Rekindle through reframing. Renew your faith in each other by reframing some earlier negative experiences by giving them a humorous look. After a couple has been married for some time, they are going to have some less than pleasant experiences in their shared history. Look back at some of those incidents, apply some forgiveness, see if you can interpret them differently and take yourselves less seriously.

Rekindle through praying. Offer thanks to God for your memories and your life together. Let God know how grateful you are for the events that make up the fabric of your marriage. Thank Him for each other and His faithfulness on Valentine's Day.

Rekindle through dining together. Plan and enjoy an elegant meal at home. While many couples go out for dinner on Valentine's Day, there's something about planning a meal, preparing it together, and enjoying it that makes love's flame grow brighter, especially if you "dress up" the meal with a nice tablecloth, your best dishes, crystal, and candles.

❧

What do you do with the children when you have this Valentine's Day meal at home? Why not include them? Tell them your stories of where you met, when and where you were married, etc. The telling will not only rekindle your love, but it will make your children feel more secure. They will be blessed by knowing Mom and Dad love each other and are committed to each other.

Love for others

While Valentine's Day may have originated with romantic love, its scope is much wider now. It is not just a holiday for lovers; it is a holiday for friends, relatives, co-workers, teachers, classmates, and other acquaintances.

A fun way we can appreciate others is by using an exercise utilized in past Valentine's celebrations. Drawing names was used to bring people together in Lupercalia and also later in England and Scotland. Young people put their names in a bowl on Valentine's Day, and then they drew names to see who their sweetheart would be.

- Cut out a small construction paper heart for each family member and/or guest. Print their names on the hearts. Place the hearts in a basket. With everyone seated in a circle, preferably around a table, ask each person to draw a heart from the basket. Let each person, one by one, offer a compliment to the person whose name was drawn. For example, if the name on my heart is Sam, I might say something like this, "Sam, you articulate yourself well. I like to be around you because the conversation is always interesting."

- Draw a person's name from those collected in a basket. Announce it and have every member of the circle respond by saying something nice about the person. Continue in this manner until each person has received his or her valentine compliments.

- Draw names for heart felt prayers. Put the names of every family member or of every guest in a basket. Shake up the names and have everyone draw a name. Then have each person to pray out loud for the person whose name they have drawn.

Love you can hold

Sending cards/or letters evolved along the way as people celebrated Saint Valentine's Day. Some sources credit this to Saint Valentine's final act before he was martyred. He sent a good-bye note to a woman who had visited him in prison and signed it "From your Valentine."

This grew to letters of love that sometimes included proposals, and then the making of cards, decorated in a variety of ways. By the 1700s, there were Valentine cards for sale. And they still are! In abundance! And in a great variety! They provide a good medium for telling others they're special, they're loved, they are being thought of, or they are appreciated.

- *Write letters* to people who are special in your life such as your children, your parents, close friends, fellow church members and perhaps co-workers and teachers. Do this as a family with an evening given over to sitting at the table, writing letters together.

End the letters with a prayer or a Bible verse you have especially selected for the recipient.

- *Make valentines* to send and to give. This can be a way your family can celebrate together. Much chatter will take place as you work together. What to say on the valentine?

  A Bible verse on each valentine, particularly John 3:16.

  "You are special because . . ."

  "You light up my life just by . . ."

  The old working stand-by, but-still-works poem: "Roses are red, violets are blue . . ."

- *Deliver valentines* you have made or bought to friends, neighbors, elderly shut-ins or nursing home residents. You might want to share some homemade heart-shaped cookies along with the cards.

- *Purchase cards* especially designed for individuals who have lost their mates in the last year. Send the cards to widows and widowers who will be experiencing their first Valentine's Day without their sweetheart.

- *Recycle valentines.* A friend of mine and I send one Valentine's Day card back and forth, writing a little note in the card along with the year. In this way, we remember each other and respect God's earth at the same time.

Whether it is expressing love, affection, or appreciation, a card or letter allows you to expressing your feelings with something the recipient can hold in his or her hand. Electronic valentines are clever and efficient, but you can hold a card, savor it, and read it again and again. It's like capturing love in the palm of your hand!

Valentine's Day cards bless people—spouses, sweethearts, friends, acquaintances, children, teachers, classmates, co-workers, and lonely people. Julia Caroline Ripley Dorr wrote about this feeling a long time ago after receiving a Valentine's Day card on a winter's day. She said, "Suddenly the cold gray skies grew soft and warm as May!"[2]

Put your heart into it

Valentine's Day is not only a time when the dark days of winter are brightened for us, but we can brighten the lives of others. Through our actions, we can show the love of Jesus.

- *Brighten the lives of widows and widowers.* Joyce Rogers writing in the February 2012 issue of *Guideposts* noticed how trying Valentine's Day for widows can be after she lost her husband of 54 years. The day was a poignant reminder of what she had lost, but then she remembered her friends who were also widows. They were probably just as lonely as she was so she invited them to her home for a Valentine's Day luncheon. Over lunch they told stories about their husbands. "The tears came," she wrote, "but so did a lot of smiles and laughter."[3]

- *Brighten the lives of children in the hospital.* If you have a children's hospital in your area or a children's wing at your local hospital, check with the volunteer coordinator and see if you can *bring* valentines to the children. Deliver them with a smile on your face or a pleasant greeting. It will lift the spirits of the patients and lift yours as well! One group takes decorated boxes with a valentine inside. The children can keep the boxes handy to store other items they receive while in the hospital—items that they might want to take home with them.

- *Brighten the lives of children in a shelter*, perhaps a homeless shelter or one for abused women. Decorate shoeboxes in valentine colors and symbols. Once the glue has tried, fill the boxes with items that might cheer a child such as small toys, coloring books, crayons and candy. Be sure to contact the director at the shelter to determine when a good time would be to drop off the boxes.

Saint appreciation

When the pope attempted to abolish the pagan festival of Lupercalia in the fifth century, he called it *Saint* Valentine's Day. The *saint* part was dropped in the last part of the twentieth century as the holiday became commercialized, but we can still recognize the value of saints.

Actually, there might have been three or even more Saint Valentines, each of whom had his feast day on February 14. All were believed to be martyrs of the Christian faith under the persecution of the Roman emperor Claudius II (A.D. 214–270).

In Claudius's time, all Christians were illegal citizens and always under suspicion because they wouldn't worship the emperor so it is possible that several valentines could have been martyred. The most prominent story, though, is about a priest who refused to support Claudius's outlawing marriage. Claudius wanted to build up his army, but married men didn't want to comply. They wanted to stay home with their wives so Claudius made marriage illegal.

A priest by the name of Valentine took pity on couples in love. He secretly married them. When his actions were discovered, he was jailed and sentenced to die. On February 14, A.D. 269, he was beheaded.

While Valentine was in jail, the jailer's blind daughter visited him, and here, too, the story varies. One variation sees their relationship as "just friends," as two people who wanted to talk, perhaps even discussing theology. Another variation sees their relationship as being romantic, and yet another version of the story says that he cured her of blindness.

While the details aren't in agreement, there are enough stories to lead us to believe a godly person existed who was willing to act on what he believed. There's enough material available to heighten our awareness of and appreciation for saints.

- Have three teens to portray three different Saint Valentines with three different stories. One could be the saint who was a friend with the jailer's daughter, one could be the saint who was in love with her, and another could be the saint he cured her. Ask others who are present to guess which one is the real Saint Valentine.

- Have three teens to portray three different saints from the Bible. Ask your children and/or your guests to guess who the saints are and tell what contributions they made to God's kingdom.

- Have your group to talk about saints among you. The New Testament recognizes as saints anyone who believes in Jesus and dedicates his or her life to following Him. Ask your family members whom they have noticed who are especially dedicated to serving God. Send them a valentine of appreciation, signing it, of course, with "from your Valentines."

Love for God

Just as Valentine's Day can be an impetus for showing our love for others, it can also be an opportunity to show our love to God.

- Make 14 (as in February 14) red hearts from construction paper. Write a number on each heart, beginning with 1 and ending with 14. Stack the hearts in the center of your dining table. The number 1 should be on top. Before the meal begins, ask family members to turn a heart over, one person at a time, and tell why he or she loves God. Don't take turns. Just let participants spontaneously reach for a heart as they think of reasons why they love God.

- A week before Valentine's Day, place some plain red paper hearts on a table in a convenient location. Add some felt tip pens and a basket. Ask family members to write on the hearts why they love God and place the hearts in the basket. At your celebration meal on Valentine's Day, bring the basket to the table, which you have covered with a white tablecloth. Scatter the hearts around the table. Look heavenward and exclaim, "God, see how much we love You." Then ask participants to pick up the hearts nearest them and read aloud what is written on them.

- Compile a song sheet of hymns and choruses that speaks to God of our love for Him such as "I Love You, Lord" or describes His love such as "Love Divine, All Loves Excelling." Then sing the words to the lover of your soul. Let Him "hear" how much you appreciate Him.
- Memorize Bible verses. One way we can show our love to God is to value His Word, to plant His Word into our hearts. When we love someone, we value what they value. Use the days up to and including Valentine's Day to focus on Scripture memory.

God's love for us

While Valentine's Day is an opportunity to acknowledge our love for others and for God, it can also be a time to acknowledge His love for us. Now that can be a real day brightener!

On red and pink construction paper hearts, copy Bible verses that speak of God's love for us. Some possibilities are John 3:16, Jeremiah 31:3, Romans 5:8, 1 John 3:1, and 1 John 4:10. Hide these hearts as if they were Easter eggs around the house. Invite the children to search for the hearts and to clap when one is found. Read aloud the verses.

If your group is made up of adolescents and adults, you might want to have the hearts scattered around on the table or one placed at each person's plate. Ask each person to read what's on his paper heart before the blessing is given. After thinking about how much God loves us, your prayer will be filled with gratitude.

Make the Bible's message personal by having verses that speak of God's love for us printed for each individual's place at the table. Ask each person to read the verse out loud but not as printed. Rather read it as a personalized message. Here are two examples.

- Jeremiah 31:3 as it appears in the King James Version says, "Yea, I have loved thee with an everlasting love; therefore with loving kindness have I drawn thee." The reader might personalize it in this way. "Yeah, God loves me with an everlasting love; therefore His love and kindness draws me to Him."

- 1 John 3:1 in the same version says, "Behold, what manner of love the Father hath bestowed upon us, that we should be called the sons of God." It could be personalized like this, "Behold, what manner of love God has bestowed upon me, that I could be called the son (or daughter) of God."

After each person has shared his personalized verse, conclude with singing "Jesus Loves Me!" or "O How He Loves You and Me." You'll be ready to sing after reminding each other of God's love for us.

What do you want Valentine's Day to be? Do you want it to be holy? If you do, you can celebrate love—your love for others, your love for God, and His love for you!

Presidents' Day

"I urge . . . that requests, prayers, intercession and
thanksgiving be made for everyone—for kings
and all those in authority" (1 Timothy 2:1–2).

On the third Monday of February, Americans honor their past Presidents with a federal holiday. Particular attention is given to George Washington, the nation's first President, and to Abraham Lincoln, our 16th President. Both men were born in February, but more importantly, both men worked very hard to make this country the *United* States of America.

Starting with George

Washington was born on February 22, 1732, and grew up on his family's farm in Virginia. As a young man, George became a skilled military leader.

At the time, America was a colony ruled by Britain. The colonists wanted to form and rule their own country. They had to fight to win their independence, and Washington led them in that fight.

As commander in chief, Washington had a challenging job. The colonists had little to work with in the way of clothes, money, food, and weapons. Washington persevered, though, and his troops respected him. They stayed loyal even when circumstances were incredibly difficult.

Eventually, the colonists were victorious, and they were able to create a free and independent country. Washington helped them write a Constitution, and the people elected him President in 1789.

As the *first* President, Washington is often referred to as the *father* of our country, and he showed this in the care and energy he gave to keeping the ideals reflected in the Constitution.

- Ask your children, What does a President do? How is he like a father? How is he not like a father?
- Ask your oldest child or your guests who were the first-born in their families, What kind of unique pressure must Washington have experienced to be the *first* President? What does being *first* entail?

As the *16th* President, Lincoln did not have the same pressure that Washington did. He did, though, have a challenge on his hands—a challenge that threatened to divide the states.

Linking with Lincoln

Born on February 12, 1809, Lincoln grew up on a farm in Kentucky, a farm much more humble than the one Washington was raised on. As a boy, Lincoln plowed fields, chopped wood, and planted and harvested crops first in Kentucky and then in Indiana.

As a young man, Lincoln moved to Illinois. There he worked splitting logs into rails for train tracks and as a store clerk. He even owned a store for a while. He had a strong interest in honesty, fairness, and justice so he become a lawyer.

His interest in fairness and justice led him into politics. When he was 25 years old, he was elected to the Illinois state legislature. This was in 1834. He became a member of Congress in 1847 and President of the United States in 1861.

Around the time Lincoln became President, the Southern states wanted to break away from the Union over the issue of slavery. Lincoln opposed slavery and so did the Northern states. Southern states wanted to keep slavery. This division led to the Civil War.

Lincoln wanted to keep America the way Washington had meant it to be. He wanted a united country run by the people, for the people, and with everyone having a chance to participate. Not everyone felt this way; some were very angered by what Lincoln said and did.

Even after the Civil War ended, with the states that were against slavery winning, some people were still angry. One of those people shot and killed Lincoln. Lincoln's leadership preserved the Union, but it cost him his life—a life definitely worth remembering.

Have a family member or a friend impersonate President Lincoln. Lincoln was a great storyteller so letting him tell his own story would be an appropriate way to remember him. A tall black top hat—and maybe a beard!—is all that is needed to get into character.

Have someone interview President Lincoln. With a microphone in hand (a wooden spoon will do!), ask the impersonator questions such as *Where were you born? What was your home life like? Did you always live in Illinois? What kind of jobs did you have? What made you run for Congress? Why did you want to be President? What was your biggest worry as President?* and *What do you see as the major contribution you made to this country?* Perhaps he will say, "I want to be remembered for keeping the United States *united.*"

United we stand

Both Washington and Lincoln believed and upheld the ideal of "one nation under God." They understood and believed in what Jesus said: "Every kingdom divided against itself will be ruined, and every city or household divided against itself will not stand" (Matthew 12:25).

After the Revolutionary War, people had many different ideas on how to be a country independent of Britain. Washington's position was that our country would fall apart if each state made its own rules. Individual states, he insisted, needed to stay together and cooperate to be strong.

By the time Lincoln became President, the states that had united were being torn apart over slavery. Lincoln worked hard to keep the states together when the southern states wanted to break away. Some people did not agree with Lincoln's thinking nor like some of his decisions, but he did what he knew was best for America.

Washington and Lincoln truly believed in the *United* States of America. Being united is a good thing, whether we are working together as a family, as a church, as a community or as a nation.

You can illustrate—and celebrate!—the strength of working together by adapting an activity from Pastor C. W. Bess. In his book *Object-Centered Children's Sermons*, he suggests using dowels (12 to 18 inches long) to explain the value of staying together. At your table, you will probably want to use 12-inch dowels. Put one at each person's plate. Also, have some string handy as you will eventually want to tie the dowels together in a bundle. Ask one person at the table to see if he can break his stick. He should be able to! Wonder out loud, "How can we make our sticks stronger?" Then acting as if you have a "flash of inspiration," tie all the sticks together, and then ask someone at the table to try to break the bundle. He shouldn't be able to. The sticks together are stronger than one alone! When we work together as a family, as a church, as a community or as a nation, we become stronger.[1]

Honest to God

Stories have been told and retold about how honest Washington and Lincoln were. Some of those stories have now been classified as just that . . . stories, but yet their circulation through the years symbolize each man's reputation for honesty.

An oft repeated story about Washington involves a cherry tree. To test a new hatchet when he was a boy, he cut down his father's favorite cherry tree. Naturally, his father was angry. Little George didn't let that faze him. He confessed he was guilty. He said to his father, "I cannot tell a lie. I cut down the cherry tree."

As a store clerk, Lincoln was meticulously honest. Late one evening when he counted the day's cash, he realized he had a few cents that was due a customer. He closed the store, and walked a long distance to make good the deficiency. On another occasion, he discovered a weight in the scales that he had used in packaging tea for a woman the night before. Looking at the weight, he realized he had not given her enough tea for what he charged her. He weighed out what was due, and carried it to her. She was surprised; she hadn't realized her purchase was short.

Applaud the honesty of these men and recognize the virtue honesty is through some table conversation inspired by holiday food.

Serve cherry pie, cherry cobbler, or cherry-covered cheesecake or a "Lincoln Log" at your main meal on Presidents' Day. A Lincoln Log could be a chocolate cake prepared in jelly-roll style with a creamy filling or a reshaping of your favorite cheese ball recipe into a log. While you nibble on pie or cheese and crackers, tell about George Washington's refusal to lie about chopping down the cherry tree or about Lincoln's carefulness to be honest in business dealings. Follow the stories with one of these exercises.

- Ask some of these questions, What commandment warns against lying? Are "white lies" harmful or are they OK to tell? What did Washington mean when he said, "I cannot tell a lie?" What would it take to be a person who "cannot tell a lie"?

- Tell a story of a time when you got caught in a lie, how you felt about it and the consequences that resulted. Ask, Why might children tell lies, especially when confronted by a parent for something they've done?

- End the meal with prayer for today's political leaders that they will be truthful men and women. Also pray for yourselves that you will be truthful in all you do.

Memory, monuments, and money

The influence, the leadership and the contributions of these two men were so important that monuments were erected in their memory. The Washington Monument in Washington, D. C., casts a long shadow as it is 555 feet tall. Near this monument in the National Mall sits the Lincoln Memorial. It is a structure that houses a large sculpture of Lincoln seated inside.

A great way to honor Washington and Lincoln on Presidents' Day would be to visit those memorials, but that is impractical for many people and impossible for others. We do, though, have "memorials" we can look at and hold in our hand: our money, for example.

A profile of George Washington appears on a quarter. President Lincoln's picture is on one side of the penny; the Lincoln Memorial appears on the back.

Washington's picture appears on one-dollar bills, and Lincoln's picture is on the five-dollar bills.

These hold-in-our-hands "memorials" can help us think about Washington and Lincoln and honor them.

Look and speak. Place pennies and quarters on the dining table. As you eat your meal together, ask, Whose faces are on the coins? What words are on the coins? What do the words mean?

Make and send. Make cards using Lincoln-head pennies. "Glue a penny on the card and use it as the beginning of a design. The penny can be the center of a flower or the head of a stick figure."[2] Send the cards as an encouragement to leaders your family admires and respects. "You're like a Lincoln in our lives. You inspire us to be honest."

Collect and share. On February 1, say to your family, "From now until Presidents' Day, let's collect money that honors Washington and Lincoln—pennies, quarters, one-dollar bills, and five-dollar bills. Let's use this money to make a contribution to missions in an area of the world where its citizens are not united and free."

Men of words

Both Washington and Lincoln are remembered for their work in building and preserving a *united* nation, but we also remember them for what they said. In their conversations and in their speeches, they said things that still have applicability today.

When it came to speaking, Lincoln was the more eloquent of the two. Washington was so nervous giving his inaugural address that his hands trembled with emotion and his voice was often inaudible. Nevertheless, he gave us wonderful axioms to ponder.

Lincoln was a master storyteller and an excellent speech maker. He worked hard at crafting his words. His most famous speech is the Gettysburg Address. It was given at Gettysburg, Pennsylvania, after thousands of soldiers had died and were buried there.

Print quotes from Washington and Lincoln on place cards or table tents. Between the main course and dessert of your holiday meal, have participants to read the quotes. Ask them to guess who said the words (I've put the author's name in brackets here) and to comment on the quote's meaning.

"We . . . highly resolve that . . . this nation, under God, shall have a new birth of freedom—and that government of the people, by the people, for the people, shall not perish from the earth."

LINCOLN

"With malice toward none; with charity for all; with firmness in the right, as God gives us to see the right, let us strive on to finish the work we are in."

LINCOLN

"I hope I shall possess firmness and virtue enough to maintain what I consider the most enviable of all titles, the character of an honest man."

WASHINGTON

"Discipline is the soul of an army. It makes small numbers formidable; procures success to the weak, and esteem to all."

WASHINGTON

"Friendship is a plant of slow growth and must undergo and withstand the shocks of adversity before it is entitled to the appellation."

WASHINGTON

More than five people at your table? Check with your library or go online for more quotes. Type "George Washington quotes" or "Abraham Lincoln quotes" in your search engine and you will have an abundance of quotes to work with.

Men of faith

Washington and Lincoln were strong leaders, men of character and conviction, and they were also men of faith. They believed in God and trusted Him.

Washington sensed that he was God's chosen vessel and that God protected him from harm. He knew victory depended on God, as the colonists did not have enough soldiers or resources to win the war on their own. Probably most telling of all with regard to his faith were the words he used when being sworn in as President. To the oath, he added four of his own words: "So help me, God." Washington depended on God.

Lincoln likewise counted on God's help. Before leaving Illinois for Washington, D. C., he said, "The task before me is greater than that which rested upon Washington. Without the help of that Divine Being who always helped him, I cannot succeed. With God's help, I cannot fail."[3]

Once while President, Lincoln asked all Americans to spend a day in prayer and fasting. He said, "It is the duty of nations as well as of men to own their dependence upon the overruling power of God, and to confess their sins and transgressions in humble sorrow, yet with assured hope that genuine repentance will lead to mercy and pardon and to recognize the sublime truth . . . that those nations only are blessed whose God is the Lord."[4]

We can use the examples of Washington and Lincoln as encouragement to work at strengthening our faith. We can do this "cherry by cherry" or "log by log."

Building your faith by gathering cherries. Print Bible references on red paper cherries. Have family members to look up the verses, read them, memorize them, and recite them. After they have recited a verse correctly, they get to put a paper cherry on a tree. You could have individual trees sketched on large pieces of heavy construction paper or you could make a large tree to post on your refrigerator.

Building faith log by log. Prepare a picture of the front of a log cabin (outline only), similar to the simple ones Lincoln lived in. The idea is to leave plenty of room for children to paste logs on the cabin. Each log could be a long paper strip or a craft stick with a Bible reference written on it. Ask the children to memorize the verses and repeat them to the group. For each memorized verse, they can add a log to complete the building of the cabin. You could make a log cabin for every child or make one large one for all the children to work on together.

Celebrate all Presidents

While the dominant emphasis in this chapter has been on President Washington and President Lincoln, your family may want to focus on several other Presidents, all of the past Presidents or the current one. All have made or are making contributions to this country.

- The faces of George Washington, Thomas Jefferson, Theodore Roosevelt, and Abraham Lincoln are carved into the rock of Mount Rushmore in South Dakota. Ask, "If you could choose four of our

Presidents to be sculpted into rock, whom would you choose? And why would you choose them?"

- Ask, "What qualities do you think make for a good President? Who among you would be a good President?" Make a large pin that says *Future President* and have him or her wear it during your Presidents' Day meal.

- Give a prayer of thanks for past leaders and ask God to give the current President strength and wisdom to serve (see 1 Timothy 2:1–2).

- Write a letter of encouragement to the current President. Tell him how much you appreciate his service to this country. You may address it to The White House, 1600 Pennsylvania Avenue NW, Washington, DC 20500.

When George Washington led his troops to pray after the French joined forces with the colonists to defeat Britain, he credited God for the victory. He added, "It becomes us to set apart a day for gratefully acknowledging the divine goodness."[5]

We already have a set-apart day. It's Presidents' Day, and on this day it "becomes us" us to honor our leaders and to thank God for His goodness and for blessing the United States of America.

St. Patrick's Day

> *Then I heard the voice of the Lord saying,*
> *"Whom shall I send? And who will go for us?"*
> *And I said, "Here am I. Send me!" (Isaiah 6:8).*

S t. Patrick's Day is a holiday that many Americans recognize and enjoy every March 17. To them, it is a celebration of Irish heritage with symbols reflective of Irish folklore and culture. Parades, partying, wearing green, leprechauns, corn beef and cabbage, pots of gold, and the blarney stone all figure in this celebration. Little is said, though, about the person for whom the day is named. For those who want to put the holy into this holiday, it pays to get to know him. There's much about his life to learn and to celebrate. For starters, he wasn't Irish!

Who was St. Patrick?

Patricius Magonus Sucatus (Patrick) was born around A.D. 389 in pre-Anglo-Saxon Britain, now known as Scotland.[1] His family was wealthy and prominent.

When Patrick was nearly 16, Irish raiders captured him along with others, took them to Ireland, and sold them as slaves.

Patrick's job as a slave was to care for sheep. "It was a grim existence, not at all like the life Patrick was accustomed to lead. Often he would spend both night and day with his flock, sitting in the chilling rain and raw bitter wind, constantly on guard for wolves or robbers."[2]

The experience, though, deepened Patrick's faith. Before his abduction, he seldom prayed. While tending sheep, he prayed frequently. Patrick's faith increased, and he sensed God's purposes at work in his captivity.

After serving six years as a slave, Patrick heard a voice in his sleep saying to him, "You do well to fast, since you are soon about to go to your own country." He wondered, *What? Did I hear right? Am I about to leave Ireland? How could this be?* After a while, he heard the message, "Look, your ship is ready."

Trusting the voice, Patrick took off even though he had no idea how he would manage. Traveling back roads and hiding much of the time, he traveled 200 miles to the seacoast, where, he discovered, a ship was ready to leave port.

When Patrick sought passage, the captain was not interested in helping a ragged and a penniless youth. He brushed aside Patrick's request. Just then several Irish wolfhounds were brought aboard ship. They snarled and snapped at their terrified handler. Patrick, who had worked with dogs for six years as a slave, spoke to them in Gaelic. His words soothed the dogs and his calmness established mastery over them. This impressed the captain! He changed his mind and allowed Patrick to earn his way home by caring for the wolfhounds.

While there is little information about the details of his escape over land, historian Leon McBeth suggests that Christians marked their humble homes with a small wooden cross so Patrick would know where to stop. "In 'underground railroad' fashion, they passed him from one Christian family to another until he came at last to the sea."[3]

Your family might want to remember Patrick's faith to believe he could escape by making a small wooden cross. Hang it on your front door to remember Patrick's courage and the Christians who helped him escape from slavery. The few Christians in Ireland assisted him when he ran away and headed for the coast to secure passage home.

Back home

When Patrick finally arrived home, he was welcomed with all the pomp and ceremony due a returning nobleman. Reunited with his family, installed in his ancestral estate, and given his father's seat in the legislature, Patrick probably never intended to stir from his native land, but God had other plans. Like the Apostle Paul, he received a call.

When Paul was in Ephesus, he "had a vision in which he saw a Macedonian standing and begging him, 'Come over to Macedonia and help us!'" (Acts 16:9 GNT). An Irishman called to Patrick in a dream. The Irishman carried letters from people in Ireland. He gave one of the letters to Patrick. When Patrick opened the letter, he heard the voice of the Irish. When he read it, the voice cried out, "We ask thee, boy, come and walk among us once more."

The voice haunted Patrick, yet he did not respond to it right away. Nine years passed before he returned to Ireland. Among the things he did during this time was go to Europe and to spend time learning about serving God and ministry. Some of those he learned from were people whose basic goal for the Christian life was total withdrawal. Patrick did not share this conviction. By nature, he was an active person, a people person, but even if he weren't, there was the call to contend with. God wanted him in Ireland.

His writings show that the imperative to "go" weighed heavily upon him. You can tell by the Bible verses he quoted, verses that you might want to print on table tents. Display the tents and read them out loud when you have your St. Patrick's Day meal.

- "Come after me, and I will make you to become fishers of men" (Mark 1:17 KJV).
- "Go ye into all the world, and preach the gospel to every creature" (Mark 16:15 KJV).
- "I will call them my people, which were not my people" (Romans 9:25 KJV).

After many setbacks and years of religious study, Patrick returned to Ireland as a missionary around A.D. 432. Although some Christians were living in Ireland—obviously since they helped him escape—it was largely pagan. Ireland was a place where magic and superstition ruled.

Patrick the missionary

The Druids formed the major religion of Ireland. This was an ancient superstition based largely upon witchcraft and nature myths. Patrick experienced steady and severe opposition from the Druids as he preached from the Bible. They tried to run him out of Ireland and kill him if necessary to get rid of him. Things got so dangerous that Patrick enlisted a bodyguard, a giant of a man and a devout Christian. He traveled with Patrick.

With preaching that was persuasive, eloquent, and biblical, Patrick won individuals from nobles to peasants. Patrick's strategy was to go first to Irish kings (village chieftains). He knew that if he could convert the kings the people would follow. When he couldn't convert the kings, he often persuaded them to allow him to preach in their districts. Gradually, his preaching converted entire tribes.

Patrick's earnestness as a missionary didn't stop with winning converts. He made sure they were banded together into strong churches. He ordained and trained clergy for those churches and also organized them together as an association.

Patrick spent about 36 years in Ireland as a missionary. When he arrived, there were only a few scattered Christian groups. When he died on March 17, 461,[4] the entire nation had embraced Christianity. Believers were banded together in strong churches, educated clergy were set over them, and adequate religious instruction was provided.

After Patrick's death, his missionary spirit remained alive; disciples of his became missionaries, preached the word, and revitalized

Christianity wherever they went. Can we continue to keep that spirit alive?

You know how some people look at seed catalogs in February, dreaming of spring and making plans for their gardens, St. Patrick's Day can be "dream time" for missions.

- What better way to honor St. Patrick—and to make this holiday holy—than to plan an outreach activity or a missions trip for the coming summer.
- Take a short missions trip on St. Patrick's Day, doing something that can be done in one day.
- Gather "a pot of gold" for missions. One of the featured symbols of St. Patrick's Day is the pot of gold, the one found at the end of a rainbow. Take a can or flower pot, paint it black, write on it in white or gold *Pot of Gold for Missions*, and set it in plain sight. Ask family members and guests to put money in it to create a pot of global gold—money to support world missions!
- Display a large world map by your dining table. Have a bunch of shamrock stickers available. Locate the places—and names— of missionaries you support and place a shamrock sticker where they serve. If you support a large group of missionaries, then be selective; use a sampling. Or spread the activity out over several days. Close this activity with specific prayers for missionaries. In Patrick's memory, you might pray for them to be revitalized in their missionary endeavors, be stronger in dealing with the opposition or to experience the fullness of the Triune God. The Trinity was an important emphasis in Patrick's work.

Patrick, the teacher

A concern of every missionary is: How do I get people to understand the Christian message? This was a concern of Patrick's. For example, how do you teach the Trinity? How do you get people to grasp that God is One but yet He is also Three?

Patrick must have had an "aha" moment as he looked around at the lush clover covering the Irish country side. A type of clover called shamrock grows everywhere in Ireland's mild, moist climate, and as he looked at it, he thought, *I can use this plant to explain the trinity.*

The shamrock's three leaves represent the Father, the Son, and the Holy Spirit. A single stem represents the Godhead joining them. Just as the Father, the Son, and the Holy Spirit are all separate and yet are one God, the leaves of the shamrock are separate yet make up one plant.

Whether this aha moment really happened, Patrick's writings showed he believed strongly in the Trinity, and acknowledging the Trinity can be a way we can put the holy into St. Patrick's Day.

Buy a pot of shamrocks to use as a living centerpiece for your St. Patrick's Day meal. Pots are readily available in supermarkets and flower shops each March. Sometime during dinner, call attention to the centerpiece. Explain how the leaf with its three-in-one leaves remind us of the separate but united parts of the Trinity.

Note the Trinity connection of the shamrock before you eat your meal. Use the last line of "Come, Thou Almighty King" as your family's prayer.

> *To Thee, great One in Three,*
> *The highest praises be,*
> *Hence evermore;*
> *Thy sov'reign majesty*
> *May we in glory see,*
> *And to eternity*
> *Love and adore.*
> FELICE DE GIARDINI

Bake and take shamrock-shaped, sugar cookies to residents in a nursing home or to church members who are homebound. Put one or two cookies (depending on size) in a clear sandwich bag. Tie with a green ribbon. Attach to the green ribbon this verse: "The grace of the Lord Jesus Christ, and the love of God, and the communion of the Holy Ghost, be with you" (2 Corinthians 13:14 KJV). This verse is one of few in the Bible where all three parts of the Trinity are referenced.

Celebrate with Story

St. Patrick's story in this chapter has been in pieces—his youth, his return home, his years before being a missionary, and his life as a missionary. Put the pieces together and share his story at your family's main meal or at a party on March 17. Make it a green party and invite guests to come, meet St. Patrick and bring a green food to share. Food options are numerous: broccoli, Brussels sprouts, green Jell-O, green beans, pistachio pudding, sugar cookies with green icing, green milkshakes, limeade or green parfaits (alternate green mint ice cream with chocolate cookie crumbs, top with whipped topping and green sprinkles).

After sharing Patrick's life story, connect his experiences with prominent Bible personalities. Have this quiz printed and placed at each plate along with a sharpened pencil.

Ask participants to circle the answer of the Bible person who matches the description. Answers are in an endnote.[5]

1. Like Patrick, he was captured and taken to another land and sold as a slave.

    Abraham   *Jacob*   *Joseph*   *David*

2. Like Patrick, he sensed God's having a purpose for his life while being a shepherd.

    Abraham   *Moses*   *Philip*   *Paul*

3. Like Patrick, he received a call in a vision to go to another country.

    David   *Philip*   *Caleb*   *Paul*

4. Like Patrick, he often encountered severe opposition in preaching the gospel.

David   *Solomon*   *Zachariah*   *Paul*

5. Like Patrick whose message was challenged by the Druids, this person's prophecies were challenged by Baal worshippers.

Joshua   *Saul*   *Elijah*   *Paul*

6. While Patrick for a time was a slave, this person considered himself a slave of Jesus Christ.

David   *Solomon*   *John*   *Paul*

7. While Patrick was a missionary to Ireland, this person was a missionary to the Roman Empire.

David   *Solomon*   *John*   *Paul*

As the party ends, and your guests are leaving, wish them an Irish blessing.

> *May the road rise to meet you;*
> *May the wind be always at your back;*
> *May the sun shine warm upon your face;*
> *May the rains fall soft upon your fields;*
> *And, until we meet again,*
> *May God hold you in the hollow of His hand.*

It's for sure you will be blessed if you adopt one of these ideas to celebrate St. Patrick's Day for you will be putting the holy into your holiday. God will be pleased.

Easter

"Go quickly and tell . . . 'He has risen from the dead.'"
(Matthew 28:7)

*E*aster is different from most of the other holidays in this book in several ways.

- It is not a national holiday declared by Congress to be observed in all 50 states.
- Its origin is holy; it was established to commemorate Jesus' resurrection. This makes it a Christian holiday although old and new cultural practices have attached themselves to this celebration.
- It is never on the same date every year. Easter is on the first Sunday after the first full moon following the first day of spring. This means it could be anywhere between March 22 and April 25.

Technically, Easter is one day—a Sunday because that's the day of the week Jesus arose, but in actuality, it is a season. Christians start thinking about Easter and its importance before the day arrives. In fact, the more you make of the season, the more meaningful and joyous your Easter Sunday will be.

The somber before the joy

The season may begin as early as Shrove Tuesday, some 47 days before Easter. This Tuesday would be followed by Ash Wednesday, Lent, Holy Week, Maundy Thursday, Good Friday, and culminating with Resurrection Sunday.

Your church may encourage you to involve yourself in all of these observances, some of them or none of them except Resurrection Sunday. To participate means focusing on Jesus, the Cross, and His suffering. This means you may experience some somber feelings, something we don't usually associate with holidays. But these feelings are not to be avoided. These pre-Easter experiences will affect the quality of your celebration on Easter Sunday. You'll be more than ready to exclaim, "He is alive!"

Your participation doesn't have to be anything major for this phenomenon to occur. When my husband and I wanted our young sons to know what Easter was really about, we brainstormed about what symbols we could put in some plastic Easter eggs. I had read a small article in *Evangelizing Today's Child* magazine about how a teacher used plastic Easter eggs to quiz her students about Jesus' last week and crucifixion. She placed representative symbols inside the eggs. She then asked each student to open an egg, take out the symbol, and tell what it stood for. Bob and I thought, *What a good idea for our family!*

The article, though, didn't list the symbols so Bob and I talked about different items we could use and scoured the house for them. We found some plastic leaves resembling palm leaves for Palm Sunday, nails for the nails that were driven into Jesus' hands, rosebush twig with a big thorn for His crown of thorns, and a rock for the stone that was rolled away from.[1] We put the symbol-filled eggs in a basket and passed it around at lunch and dinner. Every day during Holy Week, we opened eggs and talked about the symbols inside.

Perhaps it was putting our minds to work, perhaps it was searching Scripture, or maybe it was touching the thorns and the nails, but something happened to us. When Bob and I got up on Easter Sunday, we spontaneously and enthusiastically greeted each other, "He is risen! He is risen indeed!" The somber gave way to joy.

There are a number of avenues for this to happen: a giving up of something important to you during Lent, participating in a group

Bible study, reflecting on Lenten readings, attending worship services, and yes, even egg activities. The Poinsetts aren't the only ones to use eggs to move toward a joyous Easter. Many families have used eggs the same way we do, but others have taken different approaches.

Eggs-cellent ideas for Holy Week

Eggs are associated with new life, and they dominate our culture's Easter observance. They're everywhere! We can make the most of their prominence by using them to focus on Jesus. He made new life possible with His crucifixion and resurrection.

Include Bible verses in the eggs that coordinate with the symbols. Our sons knew the story of Jesus' death and resurrection so the symbols were review items for them, but if the story is vague to your family members, include a printed Bible verse along with the emblem. When a person opens the egg, she reads the verse as well as explains the symbol. Or you could include a Bible reference (chapter and verse) and not a printed verse. If you do this, have Bibles handy for each egg-opener to find the verse and read it out loud.

Read a portion of the biblical account and have children find symbols. Sometimes we need more than a verse to recall—or to learn—what Jesus experienced leading up to Easter. If this is the case, you might want to divide the story into sections. The first day have a family member read the passage out loud. After reading it, ask everyone to return the next day with a small symbol that reflects the passage or something in the passage. For example, you might start with Palm Sunday, and read about Jesus' triumphal entry into Jerusalem. Then say, "Be thinking about this story, and see if you can bring me something tomorrow to help us remember this story. Try to find something small enough to put in an Easter egg. You might find the item in your toy box or you can make something." As you gather the next day, ask family members to share their symbols and then put them in the plastic eggs. Put the eggs in a basket. Read a new section the next day and repeat the process, adding eggs to the basket each day. On Resurrection Sunday, open all the eggs, review the symbols— and the week!—and then exclaim together, "He is Risen!"

Put questions in the eggs instead of symbols. Write questions such as these on slips of paper: *Why did Jesus go to Jerusalem? What kind of meal did Jesus host for His disciples? Who denied knowing Jesus? Who betrayed Jesus? Of what crime was Jesus found guilty? Who was the governor of Judea when Jesus was sentenced to die? On what day of the week was Jesus crucified? What was something Jesus said while on the Cross?* Place the eggs in a basket. At mealtime, pass the basket around, with each person taking an egg and answering the question. The family who gave me this idea calls this activity "Easter Pursuit."

No matter which way eggs are used as a Holy Week activity, it works well because it colorful, educational, easy, and kid-friendly. This is important because dealing with crucifixion, death, and resurrection are heavy subjects and hard to explain to children. Perhaps this is why using the Easter eggs filled with symbols has been the longest running holiday tradition at our house! This is not to say that there aren't other things that can be done as we'll see, but they may involve a more "grown-up" approach.

Maundy Thursday

On Thursday night before His death on Friday, Jesus hosted the Passover meal for His apostles. This feast was the beginning of a seven-day Jewish celebration that recalled the miraculous escape of God's people from slavery in Egypt. Moses, their leader, had confronted the Egyptian pharaoh with plagues trying to get him to allow God's people to leave. The final plague was the striking of the firstborn of the Egyptians by the death angel. To have their homes spared from the death angel's work, God's people put the blood of a lamb on their doorposts. When the death angel saw the blood, he *passed over* them. Death struck the homes of the Egyptians; consequently, Pharaoh relented and allowed God's people to escape and head toward the Promised Land.

As the apostles arrived for this feast, they were chatting away about who was going to be greatest in the kingdom. They were thinking of an earthly kingdom. They didn't realize Jesus' death was imminent. In this atmosphere of misunderstanding, Jesus lovingly and thoughtfully washed their feet, ate the Passover meal with them, and instituted a new meal before heading to the Garden of Gethsemane to pray.

This "last night" or "Last Supper" shows us at least three ways we can remember this significant evening.

1. The new meal Jesus instituted was very simple. Only two elements were involved. He took bread, gave thanks, broke it, and gave it to the apostles saying, "This is my body, which is for you; do this in remembrance of me" (1 Corinthians 11:24). In the same way, with a cup of wine in His hand, he said, "This cup is the new covenant in my blood; do this, whenever you drink it, in remembrance of me" (1 Corinthians 11:25). With bread and grape juice your family can have a simple "meal" together to remember Jesus, just as He wanted us to do.

2. Another way we can remember this significant evening is to recreate the full meal Jesus had with His disciples. This feast is called a seder. It involves preparing and eating symbolic foods (an egg being one of them), having planned questions and answers, repeating psalms, singing, and even some playful activity. The seder lasts for two to three hours. Many Christians have found participating in a seder helps them better understand their Judeo-Christian history and gives them a greater appreciation of Jesus' being the sacrificial lamb whose blood covers our sin. Check online or with your public or church library for more resources on having a seder as the instructions are too extensive to include here.

3. Do I dare recommend foot washing as a way to connect with Jesus' experience on the Thursday night before His death? It would

certainly be authentic, but I can hear the reaction of some kids now! *Not me! I'm not washing anyone's feet!* But this can be a very thoughtful thing to do. It was in Jesus' time. In their climate, there were two seasons—rainy and dry. Their sandal-clad feet were either dusty or muddy so guests welcomed foot washing when they arrived at someone's home. Washing the feet of guests was good manners.

What would be the equivalent of foot washing today? Michelle Guinness in her book *The Heavenly Party* suggests that today's equivalent would be washing the cars of guests. Now that's something people might welcome!

Whether it's washing feet or cars, or something else subservient, we would be pleasing Jesus with our actions. On that long ago night, when He washed the apostles' feet, hosted an historical meal, and started a new ritual, He also gave His followers a new commandment. Jesus said, "A new command I give you: Love one another. As I have loved you, so you must love one another. By this all men will know that you are my disciples, if you love one another" (John 13:34–35). This is where the "Maundy" in Maundy Thursday comes from. Maundy is Latin for "it is commanded," and this commandment to love is one we believers are expected to follow.

Good Friday

On Friday Jesus was arrested, tried, mocked, beaten, and executed on a cross. For six hours He hung on the Cross and suffered extreme pain. To acknowledge His suffering and gain even a small appreciation of what He went through, make crosses, read words, or light candles. Or better yet, blow out the candles and experience darkness. The last three hours Jesus was on the Cross was in total darkness.

Make three crosses (one for Jesus and one for each of the thieves beside Him) from twigs, limbs, or craft sticks. Discuss the sadness of the day when Jesus was killed and what crucifixion was like. Sing the

African American spiritual, "Were You There When They Crucified My Lord?" and then hang the crosses by your front door.

Read the words Jesus spoke from the Cross. While Jesus was on the Cross, he made seven statements. Read them out loud together slowly and in a meditative manner sometime on Friday. If you wish, talk about what they mean or simply let the words speak for themselves.

- "Father, forgive them, for they do not know what they are doing" (Luke 23:34).
- "I tell you the truth, today you will be with me in paradise" (Luke 23:43).
- "He said to his mother, 'Dear woman, here is your son,' and to the disciple, 'Here is your mother'" (John 19:26–27).
- "My God, my God, why have you forsaken me?" (Matthew 27:46).
- "I am thirsty" (John 19:28).
- "It is finished" (John 19:30).
- "Father, into your hands I commit my spirit" (Luke 23:46).

Light seven candles a short while before your family goes to bed. Light them one by one as the seven statements are read. Then turn out all the house lights. Watch the candles for a bit and then extinguish them slowly, one by one, noticing the difference in the room's atmosphere as you do. In the darkness, talk about how that must have accentuated Jesus' suffering on the Cross. Thank Him for His suffering and then quietly leave the dark room.

The next morning, on Resurrection Sunday, have the seven candles burning brightly when family members arise and enter the room. Seven candles make a glowing centerpiece! Drape the candles together with some purple fabric or ribbon or cluster some spring flowers around them. As the candle centerpiece portrays light and life, this indicates that it is now time to celebrate joyously the truth that "Christ has indeed been raised from the dead" (1 Corinthians 15:20).

Easter Sunday morning

In 1732, a group of young Moravian men of Herrnhut, Germany, met regularly for prayers on Saturday night. The night before Easter, they decided that like the disciples, they would go to a place of burial. They went to a cemetery where early Easter morning they sang hymns of praise as the sun came up. This impromptu service was so meaningful that it became a Moravian custom.

When Moravians came to America, they introduced the custom here, and various Christian groups and churches have been holding sunrise services ever since. Your family might want to attend one of these, or you might want to consider having your own as we did for a few years.

I would still be hosting out door sunrise services if our family hadn't moved. We no longer have an unobstructed view of the sun coming up. Too many trees! Here are some things I've learned, though, for having meaningful outside sunrise worship experiences.

- Have a backup plan in case it rains.
- Don't have a long service especially if it is chilly. Thirty minutes works well. While people want to be present, they are often mentally groggy because they are not used to being up so early.
- Serve warm food afterward inside to encourage fellowship as attendees may be chilled from being outside.
- Don't sing really complicated songs as beautiful as they may be. Reserve those for the inside worship service at church.
- Have a short talk or even two instead of having a "message" or a sermon as you usually might expect with a worship service.
- Make the service as interactive as possible with singing, responsive readings, cheers, etc. Solos are not recommended unless they are short. Group singing works best outside.
- Some drama works. One year Mary Magdalene emerged from the small clump of trees beside our backyard and testified of what it meant for Jesus to appear to her. The disciples on the road to

Emmaus might want to show up and give you an "eye witness" account of their conversation with the resurrected Jesus (Luke 24:13–35).

- End the service with a group cheer because you have something to cheer about. Here's one we used.

    LEADER: He is risen.

    WOMEN: He is risen.

    MEN: He is risen.

    WOMEN (loud): He is risen.

    MEN (louder): He is risen.

    ALL (shout): He is risen, indeed!

Easter Sunday afternoon

After you have followed Jesus through Holy Week, joined with other Christians either at a sunrise service or a morning worship experience or both, it is time for something lighter in the way of celebration, something that expresses freedom and joy.

Release balloons. Ahead of Sunday, buy a helium-filled balloon for each person. Tie the balloons to large rocks. On Sunday afternoon, take the family outside. Remind them that a large stone was placed in front of the tomb in which Jesus was buried. But when the women went to the tomb, they found the stone gone and the tomb opened. Instruct them to untie the balloon from the rock and release it. Watch the balloons ascend and sing together the first line of "Christ the Lord Is Risen Today" or the chorus of "Low in the Grave He Lay."

Fly kites. A custom in Bermuda is to fly kites on Good Friday. This dates back to the nineteenth century when a teacher had trouble explaining Jesus' ascension into heaven so he brought his class to the highest hill on the island, where he launched a kite with an image of Jesus. When the line ran out, he cut it, and the kite flew away toward the heavens. Why not fly kites on Easter Sunday instead of Good Friday? It seems to me that it is more appropriate on Resurrection

Sunday. Instead of launching one kite, have a kite for every child. Enjoy the fun of flying them for a while before cutting the string and letting them fly away.

Create bubbles. So many great toys for playing with bubbles are available these days. Before Easter Sunday purchase some that look like long swords and purchase plenty of bubble liquid to go with them. On Sunday afternoon, hand the swords out to family members. Remind participants that Jesus' side was pierced with a sword while He was on the Cross (see John 19:31–37). Say something like this, "The piercing was to verify that Jesus was really dead. He was, but now He is alive! Let's celebrate! Let's wave our swords, see the bubbles appear and soar heavenward. Let the bubbles express the bubbling joy that is in our hearts!"

Releasing balloons, flying kites, and creating bubbles are all fun things we can do *together*, and that is as it should be. From the very first, the good news of Jesus' resurrection was meant to be shared.

Sharing the good news

When the Galilean women arrived at the tomb, they were concerned about what might have happened to Jesus. His body wasn't there. An angel answered them, "I know that you are looking for Jesus, who was crucified. He is not here; he has risen, just as he said. Come and see the place where he lay. Then go quickly and tell his disciples: 'He has risen from the dead'" (Matthew 28:5–7). As you can see, Easter calls for an active response—come, see, go, and tell.

Come, go with us. Invite friends, relatives, and neighbors to attend Easter morning worship services (usually pretty spectacular events) and then to your home to eat afterwards.

Come, play with us. Have an Easter egg party for neighborhood kids.

- Have an egg-rolling contest as a reminder of the stone being rolled away.

- Have an Easter egg hunt (naturally!) letting the children know God looks for us and wants to find us.
- Serve deviled eggs and angel food cake reminding the children that the devil entered into the person who betrayed Jesus and an angel at the tomb explained to the women that Jesus was alive.

Come and see. Invite unbelievers as well as believers to your outdoor sunrise service. When we held ours, I invited others besides our class to attend including unbelievers. On the invitation I said, "Come, see how crazy we are!" When you think about it, worshipping a God you can't see, who died and came back to life does sound crazy! As the Bible says, "For the message of the cross is foolishness to those who are perishing" (1 Corinthians 1:18). Admittedly, few unbelievers actually took me up on this invitation, but those few mattered. Plus every person who received the invitation knew that I believed in and celebrated the resurrected Jesus. And that's important to me. Is it to you?

Cinco de Mayo

"He brought us to . . . this land, a land flowing
with milk and honey" (Deuteronomy 26:9).

Cinco de Mayo, the fifth of May, is not an official holiday in the United States. It is a Mexican holiday, but it is more widely celebrated here than in Mexico. More and more Americans are becoming aware of this special day as the Hispanic population increases in the USA. As Mexican Americans celebrate, so do others, and why not? It is a vibrant, festive occasion that encourages pride and builds confidence.

Nurturing the can-do spirit

The Cinco de Mayo holiday harkens back to an eventful day in Mexican history when a battle was won when it looked like it couldn't be won. The battle was with the French, who were strong and mighty. The Mexicans at that time were weak with few resources. They hadn't recovered from a defeat 14 years earlier when they had fought the United States and lost. With a weakened army and lagging national pride, the odds were against the Mexican people defeating the French.

At that time, the government of Mexico owed money to France. The Mexicans intended to pay, but they wanted to wait a couple of years until they were stronger. The French emperor, Napoleon III, wanted his money now *and* he also wanted to conquer Mexico.

French troops captured the port of Veracruz in December 1861, then headed to the capital, Mexico City. The Mexican forces met the French army in Puebla, a city east of Mexico City. The Mexicans were outnumbered and poorly armed, but they were brave and resourceful. As the French approached, the Mexican general, Zaragoza, had an idea. Why not let loose a herd of cattle? What would happen?

Zaragoza asked his troops to gather as many bulls and cows as they could. "They let the angry animals run straight toward the French troops. Then it began to rain. Some French soldiers slid in the mud. Their carts and cannons got stuck in the deep holes. Hail started to fall. The wet weather ruined the powder needed to fire guns and cannons. The French charged up the hills three times. Each time they had to turn back. After four hours of fighting,"[1] the French surrendered. Ingenuity had saved the day.

The Mexicans won the battle, but they did not win the war. Mexico remained under French occupation until 1866, and yet the winning of the Battle of Puebla was celebrated before the war ended, and it is celebrated today. Why?

The victory is a great morale booster! It is a reminder of what the human spirit and teamwork can do. A popular refrain rising in celebration of this victory is *isi, se puede!* which means, "Yes, it can be done!"[2] It means never giving up, it means never having to accept things as they appear. It means being resourceful. We all need morale boosters like this in our lives to give us confidence that we can handle our present or future battles.

What is your particular heritage? For many Mexican Americans, Cinco de Mayo is a time to honor their heritage and celebrate it just as St. Patrick's is for those of Irish descent and Kwanzaa is for African Americans. Recalling aspects of our heritage, particularly when hard-fought battles were won strengthens us as individuals and families. What are some times in your family's history when things looked bleak as if there were no possible solutions? What battles were won when you thought for a time they might be lost? How were those battles resolved? The fifth of May can be an impetus for sharing some of your family history—either something from your lifetime or something from the life of your parents or grandparents. Nurture your family's confidence by letting them know they are of hearty stock.

What is your biblical heritage? The story of the Battle of Puebla is similar to some biblical battles in the sense that unusual methods or circumstances made the difference in the outcome.

- Deborah and Barak (Judges 4–5). When they were being oppressed by the Canaanites, God's people were terrified. The Canaanites had 900 iron chariots and other superior weapons. Deborah and Barak, though, trusted God for victory, and led the Israelites into battle. Rains fell just like it did at the Battle of Puebla. The chariots got stuck, and God's people were victorious!
- Gideon (Judges 7). With only 300 men, Gideon fought against and defeated the Midianites. Gideon's weapons? Trumpets and jars with torches inside!
- Joshua (Joshua 6:1–20). When the gates of the walled city, Jericho, were tightly shut so God's people couldn't enter the Promised Land, God told Joshua to use trumpets, shouting, and marching to unnerve the Canaanites. It worked! The walls collapsed, and God's people were able to enter the city.

Have family members look up these stories in a good Bible story book or a simple Bible translation. Ask them to study the stories and share them in their own words as you sit around the table on fifth of May.

Or have everyone read and focus on one of these stories. Notice the unusual aspects of the battle. Compare it with the Battle of Puebla, and nurture that can-do spirit that God plants in all of us. This spiritual plant needs watering from time to time, and stories like this can do that. They remind us that we always have more to fight with than we think, especially when God is with us. Now that's something to celebrate!

Fiesta time

In Mexico and in Mexican American communities, Cinco de Mayo celebrations include food, parades, folk dancing, and mariachi music. It's definitely not an occasion you celebrate alone!

If you are Mexican American, let others know who you are and what you are celebrating. I'm embarrassed to admit that when I first noticed this holiday in grocery store ads, I thought Cinco de Mayo was a person! You can tell I don't speak Spanish! I didn't know what the words meant, and I certainly didn't know the story of the Battle of Puebla. I would have welcomed an invitation to a fiesta where I could learn more. I suspect many others feel this way, particularly if the invitation includes food, storytelling, games, and music!

If you are like me (not Mexican American), Cinco de Mayo may serve as a motivation to get to know those in your area who are. Invite one or several Mexican Americans to share a meal with you. The invitation could be something like this: "Come to my house. Let's celebrate over supper. I want to hear about Cinco de Mayo and why it is important plus I want to get to know you better." You could add flavor to the mix—and the conversation—by inviting someone who has traveled to Mexico or by inviting a missionary on home assignment from Mexico. What a blend you will have—and what insight you will gain—as experiences and observations are shared.

No matter who issues the invitation, cultural sharing will take place during the fellowship, and that's what's important. We get to know each other. Through the warmth of interaction and shared food, a mellow atmosphere develops—an atmosphere just right for praying. Before the fellowship ends, ask someone to lead in prayer for those at your table, for those who don't know Jesus, for church workers who labor long and hard, for missionaries serving in Mexico, and for the crime situation along the Mexico-US border. While this holiday celebrates an actual battle, we can use this holiday to fight spiritual battles by winning friends, promoting community, praying together, and working together.

Co-laborers

Whether or not we have a Mexican heritage, we can put our heads—and hearts—together to reach others and still keep the flavor of the holiday.

Have a block party. May 5 is a good time for outdoor activities. It's not too hot and it's not too cold making it a good time to host a block party. You could do this in your neighborhood or in a section of town that is under churched. All those festive things that go with celebrating Cinco de Mayo—music, food, crafts, games, etc.—have a drawing power. People will be attracted to the sounds of a mariachi band strolling through the exhibits and food stands. As the music plays and food smells permeate the air, curiosity is aroused. People follow their noses and their ears! Have various games and interactive activities for their participation when they show up. Be sure to have plenty of gospel tracts to distribute. This way Cinco de Mayo becomes more than remembering a battle; it becomes a day for sharing Jesus.

Organize a children's parade. Parades are an important part of many Cinco de Mayo celebrations, so use a parade as a vehicle for bringing people together and sharing Scriptures. Have a noisy parade in which the sounds bring people out of their homes to see what's going on. A parade could be simple with bicycles, tricycles and scooters decorated with red, green, and white (colors of the Mexican flag) streamers. For those who walk, have them play instruments they own, blowing kazoos, or shaking maracas. Before marching, attach Scripture verses to pieces of candy. Hand out the pieces of candy with the verses attached to people who gather to watch the parade.

Host a party for neighborhood children. Invite the children for an after school party or a Saturday party, depending on what day of the week May 5 falls. At this party, you could sing, practice your Spanish, and cook together.

After Deborah and Barak's battle, they sang a victory song (Judges 5). After you tell the story of the Battle of Pueblo, lead the children in singing "Yes Lord, Yes Lord, Yes Yes Lord"[3] or "Onward, Christian Soldiers." You might want to start the singing with "La Cucaracha," a Mexican folk song about a cockroach that cannot walk. This song will delight the children, warm up their voices, and get them in the mood for some rousing singing.

Have the children make maracas to shake to add to their participation and fun. To make maracas, fill plastic Easter eggs or some other kind of plastic containers with dried beans, rice or pop corn kernels. A 16.9-ounce plastic bottle with a screw-on cap works well. You might even want the children to decorate the bottles as a party activity.

Work on saying some Bible verses in Spanish. If you don't speak Spanish, you might want to ask a student from a high school Spanish club to come to the party to assist you. Memorized verses will stay with the children and become as sweet as honey to them. To help children connect honey and God's words, make *sopaipillas* together. The children will delight in watching the pieces of bread puff out, and when filled with honey, they are delicious to eat!

HERE ARE THE INGREDIENTS FOR SOPAIPILLAS:
1¾ cups sifted all-purpose flour
2 teaspoon baking powder
1 teaspoon salt
2 tablespoons shortening
⅔ cup cold water

HERE ARE THE INSTRUCTIONS:
Sift dry ingredients into mixing bowl; cut in shortening coarsely. Add cold water gradually. Mix just enough to hold together. Turn out on

lightly floured board and knead gently until smooth. Cover and let dough rest for 5 minutes. Roll out into a 12-by-15-inch rectangle. Dough should be very thin. Cut into 3-inch squares. Drop a few squares at a time into deep, hot oil. At first, turn squares over 3 or 4 times to make them puff evenly. Fry 2 or 3 minutes on each side or until golden brown. The sopaipillas will puff like little fluffy pillows. Serve them hot with butter and honey. This recipe should yield about 20 servings.

As you munch on this honey-filled bread, this will be a good time to remind the children that God's words will add sweetness to their lives if we memorize and think about them.

> *"How sweet are your words to my taste,*
> *Sweeter than honey to my mouth!"*
> *(Psalm 119:103)*

> *"They are more precious than gold,*
> *than much pure gold;*
> *they are sweeter than honey,*
> *than honey from the comb.*
> *(Psalm 19:10)*

The Bible also refers to the Promised Land as a land flowing with milk and honey,[4] meaning a land fertile with opportunity for joyful living and serving God. We want the United States of America to be that kind of land, and it is more probable that it will be if we join understand each other, share in our celebrations and worship God together. I think we can do this. Don't you?

CHAPTER 9

Mother's Day

"Give her the reward she has earned, and let her works
bring her praise" (Proverbs 31:31).

*I*n the United States, the second Sunday in May is the day for publicly expressing love and appreciation for mothers. This is the day we thank mothers for all they do. This can mean honoring our moms, our grandmothers, aunts, stepsisters, sisters, or sometimes friends. It all depends on how wide your arms of appreciation are and who you see as deserving some recognition for being nurturing and caring.

What love prompted

We have someone who wasn't a mother to thank for this special day. Anna Jarvis of Grafton, West Virginia, dearly loved her mother. When she died in 1905, Jarvis wanted to honor her. Her mother had been a kind person who had started a women's club to help the sick and to work for peace. She was worthy of being remembered, so two years after her mother's death, Jarvis held a memorial service in Grafton.

I understand Jarvis's feelings of wanted to honor her mother. I felt the same way after my mother died. There are just some people whose life deserves more than a funeral. In my case, I wanted to sing the hymns my mother sang. I wanted to sing of my mother's faith, and I didn't want to do it alone. I organized a "Sabbath of Song" for the Saturday of a Mother's Day weekend and asked other women to sing with me.

I sent invitations to women asking them to join me for a morning at an out-of-the way country church, a place I felt would put us a little closer to heaven. I asked them to tell me their mother's favorite hymn or worship chorus when the responded. I promised, "Together we'll worship God with their expressions of faith."

I asked a friend who was a capable musician with a passion for worship to lead the singing, and we had the words of the songs printed for everyone. Interspersed among the songs, two attendees and I shared spiritually uplifting thoughts and stories about our mothers. It was truly a time of worship as we were on holy ground.

Anyone could organize something like this. You don't have to go away for a retreat. If you have a large family gathering, have some of the family matriarch's favorite hymns ready to sing or ask the mothers in attendance, What are your favorite songs? If you do this ahead of time, then you can have words and music ready for singing. The mothers will be pleased, and singing provides an activity that all ages can enjoy and participate in.

Letter writing followed

Touched by the ceremony she organized to honor her mother, Jarvis felt in her heart that all mothers should be honored. She began a campaign to get people to adopt a formal holiday to honor mothers. She wrote many letters and made many speeches.

In 1910, the governor of West Virginia responded to her efforts. He proclaimed the second Sunday in May as Mother's Day. The idea really caught on, and the next year, every state celebrated the holiday. In 1914, President Woodrow Wilson made the day official. He made Mother's Day a national holiday.

The holiday was launched to be a public expression of love, reverence, and appreciation for mothers, but the holiday became so commercialized that many, including Jarvis, ended up regretting creating the holiday. With gifts, cards, flowers, and eating out, the day has profitability stamped all over it; but if we are determined, we can still have a spiritual event.

The holy can be put into Mother's Day with thoughtful activities that truly honor mom such as personalized greeting cards and special awards, by looking at mothers in the Bible, and by studying Scriptures related to mothering. We can make this a day when mothers can truly feel valued and supported.

Personalized greeting cards

There are some amazingly beautiful cards with rich sentiment in stores, but no card will be treasured as one you make. With scraps of paper, pictures from magazines, sequins, and ribbons, create cards especially for Mom.

- For the greeting inside the card, finish statements such as "I love you because . . ."; "You are a supermom because . . ."; "You make me feel good when . . ."; or "My favorite thing that we do together is . . ."
- Cut out a teddy bear shape out of card stock or construction paper. Decorate it with markers, crayons, and colored bits of paper. Write on it *Good for Free Bear Hugs* and then give it to Mom.
- Stumped for words? Take one of the many statements made by that prolific author "Unknown" and use it as the sentiment or verse for your home-crafted card.

A man's work is from sun to sun,
but a mother's work is never done.

Of all the special joys in life,
The big ones and the small,
A mother's love and tenderness

Is the greatest of them all.
God could not be everywhere,
so He created mothers.

- Make a list of the words you could use to describe your mother and give her a "flower of words." Cut out a circle for the flower's center and write in the middle of it, *Mother is . . .* Cut out petals, a stem, and leaves. On each petal, write a word about Mother. Paste flower, stem, and leaves on a big piece of colored paper. On the leaves, write *Happy Mother's Day* and present Mom a bouquet of words.

Admittedly, these card ideas appear to be for children, and you might help children make cards for their mothers. Adults, though, can make personalized greeting cards too. My husband has been honoring all of us through the years with cards he has made from clipping pictures and captions from magazines. Bob's homemade cards are so personal and clever that we much prefer them over commercial cards.

"Give her the reward she has earned"
(Proverbs 31:31).

Besides honoring her own dear mother, Anna Jarvis started a campaign for a national Mother's Day because she believed adult children neglected their mothers. In the many letters that she wrote, she explained her idea. She said, "This should be a day to honor the best mother who ever lived—*your* mother." When we think of *the best*, we think of special awards. Honor the mother at your house with a special award.

Mother of the Year Award. Have an award ceremony with family members listing Mom's accomplishments and singing her praises. Present her with a home made trophy inscribed with *Mother of the Year* and the date.

Supermom. Hold an award ceremony with family members verbalizing Mom's accomplishments that earned her this special award. Present her with a certificate bearing the word *Supermom*.

Bless her for being "The Best." "Many women do noble things," but let your mother know that in your eyes, "you surpass them all" (Proverbs 31:29). Before the meal that will honor Mom, usually Sunday breakfast or dinner, gather family members together and compose a blessing. Begin this way, "God, bless our mother . . ." At the meal, read the blessing together. Save the blessing and use it year after year, making it a Mother's Day tradition.

First Place Winner. When Olympic winners are honored, they are given a medal to hang around their necks and a bouquet of flowers. This works for honoring moms, too, for the herculean work they do. Remember, Mom's work is never done! Make a medal for her: Print *First Place in Our Hearts* on a medallion (made out of a juice can lid) and tie it to a rope, a ribbon, or a long shoestring. When you present the medallion to her, also give her a bouquet of carnations, the official Mother's Day flower. If her mother is living, give her red or pink carnations. If her mother has gone to heaven, give her white carnations. Or if you prefer, give the award-winning mom a bouquet of her favorite flowers. She'll be impressed that you know her favorite!

Mothers in the Bible

For some reflective fun at the dinner table, maybe while having desert, take a quiz or two.

Quiz Number One. This quiz is about famous sons and their mothers in the Bible. These men are readily recognizable, but do we know their mothers? Match the sons with their mothers, and see if this can spark some discussion about the traits of mothers. Answers are found in the endnotes.[1]

_____ 1. Jesus   A. Sarah

_____ 2. Cain and Abel   B. Elizabeth

_____ 3. Isaac   C. Mary

_____ 4. Jacob   D. Eunice

_____ 5. Joseph   E. Jochebed

_____ 6. Moses   F. Hannah

_____ 7. Samuel   G. Eve

_____ 8. Solomon   H. Rebekah

_____ 9. John the Baptist   I. Bathsheba

_____10. Timothy   J. Rachel

Quiz Number Two. Here's another Bible quiz, looking at mothers from a different vantage point. Circle the correct answer. Answers and Bible references are in the endnotes.[2]

1. Who is known as "the mother of all living"?
   A. Eve   *B. Sarah*   *C. Rebekah*

2. What mother instructed her young son so thoroughly that Paul said, "From a child thou hast known the holy scriptures"?
   A. Dorcas   *B. Priscilla*   *C. Eunice*

3. What mother helped her son deceive his old, nearly blind father?
   A. Rebekah   *B. Rachel*   *C. Leah*

4. What mother dedicated her first son to God to serve in the tabernacle?
   A. Rachel   *B. Hagar*   *C. Hannah*

5. What mother was sent out into the wilderness with her little son because the "other wife" in the household was jealous?
   A. Rachel   *B. Hagar*   *C. Hannah*

6. What mother asked Jesus that her two sons might have the places of honor at His right and left sides in His kingdom?

   A. Widow of Nain   *B. Peter's mother*   *C. Zebedee's wife*

7. What disciple did Jesus ask to care for His mother at the time of His crucifixion?

   A. Peter   *B. James*   *C. John*

8. What mother's son was raised to life by Jesus?

   A. Widow of Nain   *B. Peter's mother*   *C. Zebedee's wife*

9. Whose mother did Jesus cure of a bad fever?

   A. Peter   *B. James*   *C. John*

10. What mother asked her daughter to ask for the head of John the Baptist?

   A. Salome   *B. Herodias*   *C. Lois*

Scriptures related to mothering

The Bible is rich in references appropriate for quoting when honoring mothers. Two of those references are Proverbs 31:10–31 and Psalm 139:7–10.

1. While the Proverbs passage is about a godly wife, this woman is also a mother (see 31:28). One of her characteristics is that she "speaks with wisdom, and faithful instruction is on her tongue" (Proverbs 31:26). Just what is this wisdom that mothers have? They point us in the right direction, instruct us how to act, and motivate us to take action. They have often do this through wise sayings that are repeated over and over.

⬥

Type up a few of the sayings associated with mothers and make copies for each person, something similar to this:

Mothers' words of wisdom

The women who nurture us often have tidbits of sagely wisdom that they freely offer. Here are some of the things they say. Check the ones your mother (or grandmothers) used or uses.

_____ Haste makes waste.

_____ A rolling stone gathers no moss.

_____ Cleanliness is next to godliness.

_____ Love makes the world go around.

_____ Sleep tight, don't let the bedbugs bite.

_____ If the shoe fits, wear it.

_____ I have eyes in the back of my head.

_____ When life hands you lemons, make lemonade.

_____ Laughter is the best medicine.

_____ Actions speak louder than words.

_____ If at first you don't succeed, try, try again.

_____ Keep your words sweet as you may have to eat them.

_____ Don't talk with your mouth full.

_____ If you can't say something nice, then don't say anything at all.

_____ If it's worth doing, it's worth doing well.

_____ The early bird catches the worm.

_____ Don't cry over spilled milk.

_____ You can do anything you set your mind to.

Hand out this printed exercise along with pencils as you clear the table and get ready to serve dessert. Share the results with each other, recognize the wisdom of mothers and enjoy their insights as you eat dessert together.

2. The classic children's book *The Runaway Bunny* by Margaret Wise Brown seems to be especially made for Mother's Day. The little bunny tries in many ways to get away from his mother, but she is "always there." It's a good read-aloud book.

- One person may read it out loud—the mother to the children or the child to a mother.
- Or two people can read it our loud, with one person taking the voice of the mother rabbit and the other the voice of the runaway bunny.

And then while the family is still sitting close listening after the reading, direct their attention to this part of Psalm 139.

"Where can I go from your spirit?
Where can I flee from your presence?
If I go up to the heavens, you are there;
If I make my bed in the depths, you are there.
If I rise on he wings of the dawn,
If I settle on the far side of the sea, even there your hand
will guide me, your right hand will hold me fast"
(Psalm 139:7–10).

The psalmist comes to the same conclusion that the bunny did, God is with us wherever we go. This is something that mothers may need to be reminded of as well as children.

Ministry to Moms

Mothering is a vital role, an important role, but fulfilling this role can be challenging and at times even discouraging. All mothers—whether they are physical or spiritual moms—need encouragement from time to time, and some moms in particular.

Single moms. Do you know a single mother with small children? What can you do to make Mother's Day special for her? Give her a basket of luxury bath items plus an offer to take the kids to the park so she can have a long, uninterrupted soak in the tub. Or perhaps you could invite her and her kids to share a Mother's Day meal with your family.

Women who've recently lost their moms. What a tender time the first Mother's Day without Mom is! You might want to include the woman with a fresh loss in her life to your family meal, ask her to sit by you at church, or call her late in Sunday afternoon after the festivities at your house are over. Get a couple of ice-cream cones, go sit in a park somewhere, ask her what her mother was like and shed some tears with her.

New mothers. Ask all the mothers and grandmothers in your extended family or church group to respond to this question, "What advice would you offer a new mother?" Record their answers on paper, put them in an album or folder and give them to a new mother.

Forgotten moms. Visit mothers in homes for older people or rehabilitation centers. Take a bouquet of carnations with you, and walk through the halls, looking for those women whom no one has visited on Mother's Day. Give each one a carnation and ask her to tell you about her children or her mother.

When we celebrate Mother's Day, we are pleasing God because the Bible encourages us to honor her (Exodus 20:12; Ephesians 6:2–3). Of course, we should honor mothers in the sense of being respectful and appreciative all year round. But in the busyness of life, in handling numerous responsibilities, we don't always do this. Mother's Day means it's time for her children to "arise and call her blessed" (Proverbs 31:28).

Memorial Day

"These stones are to be a memorial
...forever" (Joshua 4:7).

*W*hat are those stones?" asked seven-year-old Joel. He
didn't mean rocks alongside the road; he was referring to
large, mostly gray tombstones. We had just moved to a house in the
country where we had to pass a cemetery to get there. Joel's question
was one of many that I answered about the cemetery.

I explained to Joel that a tombstone was a grave marker. It
showed that someone had lived, died, and was buried there. The
stone was a memorial to the person. This prompted him to ask,
"What is a memorial?"

"A memorial is something that helps us remember or prompts
us to recall significant people or events. It could be an object. It could
be a speech, a letter, a song, or even a day. Every year in the United
States, we have a day set aside for remembering. It's called Memorial
Day, and that's when we visit cemeteries, look at tombstones, and
decorate graves. It's a day that began as a way to remember soldiers
who had died. Now it prompts us to remember others as well."

In the beginning

Memorial Day, celebrated the last Monday in May, began out of a
sentiment similar to that of God's people when they established the
feast of Purim. The Jews in Persia would have been wiped out if it

hadn't been for Esther's risking her life. Aware of what a close call they had, and how God had protected them through Esther's intervention, they wanted never to forget. They concluded that the days of Purim should "be remembered and observed in every generation by every family, and in every province and in every city. And these days of Purim should never cease to be celebrated . . . , nor should the memory of them die out among their descendants" (Esther 9:28).

The people of the United States hadn't been close to extinction, but they had suffered deeply and came close to splitting during the Civil War (1861–65). When it was over and the *united* states were still in tact, people were horrified by the cost of the war to both the North and the South. The fighting had been gruesome, bloody and ugly. Thousands of Americans on both sides died in combat. As people grieved the tremendous losses, people began visiting the graves of soldiers and leaving flowers as if to say we will never forget what you did.

Not everyone did this at first; it simply didn't occur to them, but when some people started decorating the graves of soldiers, the practice spread. The effort gave them something to do at a time when they felt like there wasn't much they could do.

Decorating continues to be a lovely way for the living to honor the dead—for all those who have lost their lives in military service and for our own loved ones and friends who have passed on. Decorating their graves is a way of saying, "We'll never forget you."

- Prepare flowers to take to graves on Memorial Day. This could be flowers from your garden, flowers you purchase, or artificial floral arrangements made especially for adorning graves.
- Make small crosses to take. Crosses can be crafted out many items—craft sticks, yard sticks, cardboard, and even egg cartons. Cut an egg carton into two sections—one with six cups and the other with five. Glue the middle cup of the five-section piece inside the second cup of the other piece and you will have a cross to paint or decorate.

- Buy small flags to take. These are inexpensive and readily available at discount and dollar stores.

By taking your children to a cemetery and decorating graves with any of these items or a combination of these items, you will see that the memory of your heroes, your ancestors, and your loved ones will not die out. You will perpetuate their "memory through all generations" (Psalm 45:17).

Flowers to remember, flowers to heal

While the intent of decorating the graves of Civil War soldiers was to remember them, the act also helped Americans heal. Many were struggling with the residue of war—grief, anger, bitterness, confusion, etc. They felt separated from the "other side." While the outcome was that the United States was still united, people didn't feel united. But accounts of people here and there decorating the graves of both the Blue (the North) and the Gray (the South) began healing the breach and would eventually lead to the formation of Memorial Day.

One of those accounts involved a group of women who went to a cemetery in Columbus, Mississippi. Soldiers from both the North and South were buried there. They laid flowers upon the graves of the Southern soldiers laid to rest there. After finishing their graves, the women then placed flowers on the graves of Northern soldiers. As the women honored soldiers from both sides, a group of Union soldiers still around for reconstruction saw the women moving from grave to grave. The men were touched and told others who told others. Eventually the story of the women's honoring the graves of all soldiers appeared in the *New York Tribune*. Reading the story inspired Francis Miles Finch to write the poem, "The Blue and the Gray."

You'll be able to find a copy of this poem at many Internet sites. Just type "The Blue and the Gray" poem into your search engine, and many options will appear. Here are the third and last stanzas.

From the silence of sorrowful hours
The desolate mourners go,
Lovingly laden with flowers
Alike for the friend and the foe;
Under the sod and the dew,
Waiting the judgment day;
Under the roses, the Blue,
Under the lilies, the Gray.

No more shall the war cry sever,
Or the winding rivers be red;
They banish our anger forever
When they laurel the graves of our dead!
Under the sod and the dew,
Waiting the judgment day,
Love and tears for the Blue,
Tears and love for the Gray.

Here are some ways you could use this poem as a part of your Memorial Day celebration.

- Read out loud together these two stanzas before your family eats their main meal on Memorial Day.
- Ask someone who is a good reader to read the whole poem aloud.
- Have copies of the poem available for everyone and make it a responsive reading. Ask someone to be the lead reader. He or she would read the first four lines of each stanza. The whole group would respond by reading the lines, "Under the sod and the dew, waiting the judgment day." These two lines appear in every stanza. The last two lines in each section end with something about "the Blue" and "the Gray." Assign half of your group to read the lines about "the Blue" and the other half to read the lines about "the Gray."

Incidents like this one about the Mississippi women spread and caught on. To decorate the graves of soldiers who died on both sides just seemed like the right thing to do. As a result, some states began setting aside a special day for doing this yearly; other states followed. This sentiment launched Memorial Day, only it wasn't called Memorial Day. It was called Decoration Day, which seems most appropriate don't you think?

From decoration to memorial

In 1866, an early veterans association suggested May 30 as the yearly date for decorating graves of soldiers who died in the Civil War. In 1882, the name was changed to Memorial Day as the observance came to be more than putting flowers on graves. In 1948, Memorial Day became a national holiday. By this time, with other wars having been fought, it became a day to remember Americans who died serving in any war. To remember them means visiting cemeteries.

Visit and decorate. Follow the original purpose of this holiday by decorating the grave of someone killed in action. The grave you decorate could be of a soldier you have known who has died in Iraq or Afghanistan in the last 15 years. It could be someone from long ago such as a grandparent or uncle who was killed in war, someone you want your children to know about. If you know of no one, look for a neglected grave and put flowers there to remember this unknown-to-you soldier.

Visit and pray. Express gratitude while you are at the grave of the soldier. Thank God for his or her service and for the freedom you currently experience.

Visit and read. President Lincoln gave a speech at Gettysburg where so many Civil War soldiers were killed and buried. He explained what the men had died for, so reading the Gettysburg Address in a hallowed place honors their memory.

Visit and explore. Help your children develop an appreciation of the past—connecting yesterday with today—by giving them paper and pencil. Ask them to make etchings of the tombstones with interesting designs. If your children hold the paper over the stone and rub the side of the pencil lead back and forth across the paper, the designs will appear on the paper. As you return home, you can talk about the designs and post the etchings on your refrigerator.

As you decorate, pray, read or explore in a cemetery where the green grass provides a lovely backdrop to the decorated graves, you will sense that God is approving, that you are doing the right thing by honoring those who've lived and sacrificed. You will experience the blessing that comes by remembering the righteous (see Proverbs 10:7).

Remembering soldiers and others

As people remembered soldiers who had died serving this country, they couldn't help but remember other people who died. The result was that Memorial Day eventually evolved to remembering others besides soldiers and in remembering them in other ways besides going to cemeteries.

Help plan a Memorial Day church service by remembering members who died in the last year. In large churches where a paid staff plans the worship service this may not be an option, but in smaller churches, the pastor may welcome the help. Ask families of the deceased to bring in pictures of those who died. Display the pictures around the altar. Print placards to go by their pictures, stating who they are and whose family they are a part of. Instead of displaying framed pictures, you might want to make a DVD and play it during the worship service.

Write notes of remembrance to families you know or who are in your church who have lost a loved one in the past year. It's a comfort and a blessing to know that someone else remembers. When Joel was eight, on Memorial Day, he asked to take a flower from our yard to the cemetery—the one he had so many questions about. A boy in his class had died that year of cancer and was buried there. When Joel arrived, the mother of the boy was there. She beamed when she saw Joel; her eyes filled with tears. A classmate had remembered!

Create a home memorial. If you have lost a relative or family friend in the last year, ask your children to gather items that remind them of the person. Use items such as a Bible, a handmade item, a favorite key chain, and a piece of jewelry to make a centerpiece or display them on a table with a picture of the deceased.

Make a family memory book. In her book *Holiday Fun Year-Round,* Dian Thomas suggests that Memorial Day is a good time for starting a Family Memory Book. She writes, "Make a page for each family member who has died. Use a loose-leaf binder so that you can add pages each year."[1]

"Write down the facts at the top of the page, including their name, where and when they were born and died, and how they were related to you. If they had a spouse or children, also include their names. Then write things you or another member of the family can remember about that person and what made them special."[2]

This is another way of perpetuating the memory of generations plus if you bring the book out and add to it each year it will turn into a legacy for your family. As family members look through it, they will be reminded of who they are, of what kind of stock they are made, and what values your family holds dear.

Launching summer

On June 28, 1968, President Lyndon B. Johnson signed legislation shifting the dates of certain holidays to provide Americans with an increased number of three-day weekends. One of those shifts was changing Memorial Day from May 30 to the last Monday of May. With that shift, a change in the celebration occurred that eliminated much of the solemnity. It came to stand for the first big fun opportunity of the summer—the first chance to "get away" or for getting together with friends and family out-of-doors. Nevertheless, remembering is still possible.

Expand the blessing. Everyone knows there is going to be good food at a family picnic. Before the blessing, remind the group what the day is about. Speak the names of any family members who died in the last year. Pause and let the names sink in. Then say, "We remember these loved ones and what they contributed to our family, to our church, to our community. Let's thank God for their lives as we thank Him for this delicious food."

Make a centerpiece of stones. God instructed His people to build a stone memorial when they crossed over the Jordan River to enter the Promised Land (see Joshua 4–5). God parted the water for them making this crossing possible. He told them to gather stones from the river to form a memorial so they would always remember what God had done.

If you are at home, at the beach, or in a park for Memorial Day, have your children gather flat stones. Ask your gatherers to print on the stones the names of people they have known who died in the last year, of family members who are no longer living, and/or of people who died in military service. Have a shallow tray or plate on the table ready to hold the rocks. In the center of the tray place a small American flag. Ask family members to read the names on their rocks and place them in the tray right before the blessing of the meal.

Pause for remembrance. Whether you are home, whether you are at a park or whether you are traveling, you can pause for a moment to remember at 3:00 P.M. A National Moment of Remembrance resolution was passed in 2000. At 3:00 P.M. local time all Americans are asked to voluntarily and informally observe in their own way a moment of respect, pausing from whatever they are doing for a moment of silence. If you are in the car, ask everyone to be quiet. If you are on the beach, ask everyone to sit for a time, to close their mouths, and even their eyes. If you are at a picnic, call everyone together, perhaps make a circle, holding hands for a moment of silence.

Memorial Day means honoring those who died in service to this country, remembering family members and other loved ones who have died, and launching the beginning of summer activities. Many of our holidays are like this; they have multiple emphases. That's why putting the holy into holidays means being intentional about the way we celebrate! It's making sure we care enough to have celebrations that matter.

CHAPTER 11

Flag Day

"May there be shouts of joy when we hear the news
of your victory, flags flying with praise to God
for all that he has done" (Psalm 20:5 TLB).

What's your vote for the number one symbol of the United States? Would you vote for the bald eagle, the Liberty Bell, the Statue of Liberty, the Great Seal of the USA, Uncle Sam, or the flag? I'd vote for the flag because this is the one symbol we've set aside a day to honor. Every June 14 is Flag Day. No other symbol gets that kind of attention. Isn't it amazing that a piece of cloth could be so important?

Need for a flag

Flags came into use so that soldiers could tell where their leader was on crowded battlefields. Wherever a soldier was, he knew where his commander was by sighting the flag.

Over time the significance of the flag increased. It went from standing for the leader's location to standing for the leader himself and for the group's motivation. A flag could rally the troops. Eventually the flag came to stand for their land and people, and every country had its own special flag.

George Washington felt we needed our own flag when we were fighting for independence from Britain. At the time we were subjects of Britain; we had their flag. We needed something that represented us.

Others felt that way too. The colonists developed and used lots of different flags during the Revolutionary War. Some looked like the British flag with colors of red, white and blue. Another showed a snake over the words *Don't tread on me.* One had the word *liberty* spelled out on it.

- If you had been part of the 13 colonies seeking independence from Britain, what would you have wanted the flag to look like? What colors would you have used? What images would you have put on it?
- What did the words *Don't tread on me* and *liberty* say about the spirit of the British colonists?
- What kind of design would you use for a flag that represents you and particularly your faith?
- What would a family flag look like? What images would represent your family? My husband suggested a poinsettia and an Easter lily for our images. Pretty good representations for a Christian family whose last name is Poinsett, don't you think?

As your table conversation will illustrate, a flag can be designed in numerous ways. When we are part of a group—a nation, a family, a faith community—we need to agree on a design that will unite us, inspire us, and remind us who we are and what we stand for. A flag is more than a piece of cloth to wave in the air.

Meaning in the design

Once the Revolutionary War was won, the 13 colonies needed a flag to unite and represent them. They needed *one* flag—the same flag for everybody. What would this flag look like? What would it stand for?

It was important that they have a different flag than that of the British since they were now independent of them. It was also important that the flag represented the 13 colonies that were banding together to make a new nation. Consequently, 13 figured prominently in the development of the flag. On June 14, 1777, the nation's leaders decided the flag would have 13 red and white stripes and 13 white stars on a blue background. This way a star and a stripe would represent each state.

This didn't mean that every state pictured the flag the same way. Congress chose the colors, the stars, and the stripes, but Congress did not say where the stars and stripes had to go! The result was a variety of flags—all red, white, and blue but with different looks.

- For the fun of it, give your family members a certain number of stripes and stars and ask them to arrange them on an 8½-by-11-inch flag. See what diverse arrangements you get.
- Or give your family members several pictures clipped from magazines that might represent your family (a boat, a house, a certain tree, the Bible, a flower, a bird, a goblet, a cross, etc.). Ask them to design a family flag. Show your flags to each other and talk about the various patterns.

George Washington drew a picture of what he wanted and took the picture to Betsy Ross, a seamstress who made clothes and sometimes flags.[1]

She made some changes in Washington's design, and then she showed the picture to him. Washington liked what he saw. Betsy Ross got busy and made the flag according to her design—blue in the corner, and the red and white stripes going horizontally. The flag she sewed became the first official flag of the United States, but unforeseen to her—and to Washington—there would be a problem with the design.

Growing country, growing flag

If the flag's symbolism was to remain the same, with a star and a stripe, for every state, the flag was going to grow as new states formed. As people moved west and the government acquired more land, each new state meant 1 more star and 1 more stripe to add. By

1818, the United States had 20 states. Can you imagine what a flag with 20 stripes and 20 stars might have looked like? Along with the crowded look was the realization that this flag could get bigger!

Consequently, American leaders decided the flag would always have just 13 stripes. These would stand for the first 13 colonies. Only a star would be added for each new state after that. That's why today's flag has 50 stars for 50 states, and 13 stripes for the original 13 colonies.

Flag Day reminds us to pause from our routines and take a closer look at our flag. When we do, we can see our beginning, some of our history, and our current status.

- Point out the parts of the flag and talk about what the stripes and stars stand for. Explain that the red stands for bravery, the white for purity, and the blue for justice. We always need to be reminding those we celebrate with what our symbols mean. Otherwise, their significance can get lost.
- Compare the symbols on the flag with the symbols on the Great Seal of the USA. You'll be able to find pictures of the Great Seal on the Internet. What does the seal have that our flag doesn't have?
- What are the symbols of the Christian flag? What do they stand for? How are the symbols on the Christian flag different from those on the American flag?

Inspired by the American flag

In 1897, Charles C. Overton was a Sunday School superintendent in New York State. When the guest speaker for his Sunday School kickoff didn't show up, Overton had to speak. Grappling for something to say, he spied an American flag near the podium. He started talking about flags and their symbolism. It occurred to him that Christians should have their own flag, and he shared his idea with the audience.

Whether the audience remembered the idea, Overton did. The idea of a Christian flag stayed on Overton's mind long after his speech. Ralph Diffendorfer, secretary of the Methodist Young People's Missionary Movement, liked the idea. In 1907, Overton and Diffendorfer teamed up to produce and to promote a Christian flag.

Compare the American flag and the Christian flag. How are they alike? How are they different? What are the symbols of each? What do the symbols stand for?

Compare and contrast the pledges to each flag. Here are the pledges.

I pledge allegiance to the Flag of the United States of America and to the Republic for which it stands, one Nation under God, indivisible, with liberty and justice for all.

I pledge allegiance to the Christian flag, and to the Savior for whose kingdom it stands; one brotherhood uniting all mankind in service and in love.[2]

What differences do you see in the pledges? What similarities? One similarity is that they both promote loyalty when we repeat the words, and this is something we want to make sure we do on Flag Day. There's no better way to honor our flag than to thoughtfully and sincerely pledge our allegiance, and to do that, we need to be looking at a flag.

What so proudly we hail

Flag Day means displaying the flag. Some communities line their main street with flags; some neighborhoods do too. It is an inspiring sight to see. Point out the many flags to your children, remind them of the special day that it is.

Maybe you are fortunate enough to have your own flag pole, where you can hoist the flag, and see it waving in the breeze. Your act will bless others in your neighborhood and will speak to your children, particularly if you make the hoisting a family affair. Once the flag is up, stand back, look at it, salute it, and say the pledge together.

If you don't have a special bracket for holding a flag, and you want to let the Stars and Stripes shine from your house, try a new wave for Old Glory.

- Place small inexpensive flags on your lawn.
- Place small flags by your mail box.
- Line your driveway with flags.
- Put several flags in a flower pot.

If you cannot display flags outside (you don't have a lawn or a porch), place a flag or flags somewhere inside.

- Make door hangers decorated in red, white, and blue and hang on the doors in your apartment.
- Buy miniature flags and stick them in cupcakes iced in red, white, and blue. Have a cupcake at each person's plate at the table.
- Have a table centerpiece of red, white, and blue carnations with two or three flags included.

As you gather around your table, say a prayer. Flag Day is a reminder to thank God for our country, to seek His help in being loyal and true, and to ask him to keep our country free with our flag flying high and unhindered.

O Say, Can You Sing?

We can strengthen the effect of our flag displaying, pledging, saluting and praying by singing patriotic songs. Singing adds feeling to the activities, making them more meaningful and their effect more lasting. In a sermon, Paul W. Powell described what singing along side the pledge did for him as a boy. Every week the whole school met for an assembly that began with the pledge and the singing of "America the Beautiful." He said, "I did not know much about America. . . . I did not understand our system of government. I was not aware of America's place in world affairs. I had little understanding of the problems that we were facing as a nation. . . . But as we pledged the flag and as we sang that great hymn I felt I was a part of something great and good. And there stirred in me feelings of pride and joy and gratitude."[3] And we want to stir these same feelings in our families as we celebrate Flag Day. We can sing this same song as we display our flag or we could sing one of these.

- "America" ("My Country, 'Tis of Thee")
- "Battle Hymn of the Republic"
- "God Bless America"
- "God Bless the U.S.A." ("I'm Proud to Be an American")
- "This Land Is Your Land"
- "The Star-Spangled Banner"

If your family finds it hard to sing "The Star-Spangled Banner"— and this wouldn't be anything unusual—make photocopies of the song and place one at each plate as you eat together on Flag Day. Read the words together. Ask, What words jump out at you? Is there something in the song you haven't noticed before? What does "Praise the Pow'r that had made and preserved us"[4] mean? What motto is expressed in the song? Would the motto still be a good one to live by today or is it obsolete?

If your family does not know the story behind "The Star-Spangled Banner," you might want to use Flag Day as an opportunity to tell it because it illustrates the power of the flag.

In 1812, the United States was at war with England once again. It was a devastating and discouraging time for Americans. The British infiltrated our land, sailed up our rivers, marched down our streets, and even burned the White House. As the war dragged on, British soldiers bombed a fort in Maryland. In September 1814, Francis Scott Key watched the fighting all through the night. He was worried and fearful as British rockets whizzed in the air. What if American soldiers gave up? What if we lost the fort?

It was a long night, but in the early morning light, Key saw the "broad stripes and bright stars" flying above the fort! The Americans had won the battle!

Key was so relieved and proud that he wrote a poem about the victory and seeing the flag over the fort. Later his poem was put to music and sung. The song caught on and eventually became our national anthem.

As powerful as this war song is, it doesn't mean our flag is just about war. While soldiers have carried it into battles, explorers, athletes, artists, and scientists have carried our flag too. Its bright colors fly at baseball games and other sporting events. It even stands proudly on the surface of the moon! Two American astronauts placed it there in 1969.

The question for us is, Is it displayed at our homes on June 14? Is it stirring our hearts? Flag Day reminds us that it should be, and we might not have this yearly reminder if it hadn't been for children saying "Happy Birthday" to the flag.

A child — or rather children — shall lead them

In 1885, when the US flag was 108 years old, Bernard Cigrand, a teacher in Wisconsin had an idea. *Why not have a birthday party?* His students liked the idea, and so they celebrated the flag with a party. You might say this was the first Flag Day.

When George Balch, a New York City teacher, heard about it, he and his kindergarten students also had a party.

Balch told those in charge of the New York schools about their flag party. The school leaders liked the idea so much that they asked all their schools to observe a Flag Day. This was in 1889. The idea spread. In 1894, 300,000 children in Chicago observed Flag Day.

June 14 is still a good time for children to have a flag party. Invite others to your Flag Day party—other families, children in your neighborhood, children in Bible clubs, or children from a missions group. Since Flag Day occurs in June, make your party an outdoor one and play "Capture the Flag." This game is one all ages can play, and it will help children understand the concept of rallying around and defending a flag.

For this game, you will need a large area which can be roughly divided into two sections and two flags of different color or design. You don't want to use the American flag for this game, as it wouldn't be appropriate. The flags just need to be something soft and pliable, something that could be picked up easily from the ground and taken back to the other section.

Split the group into two teams and assign one section of the play area to each team. Each team chooses a base position, where they keep their flag, and a jail position, where they will keep their prisoners. Each team tries to capture the other team's flag. Whenever a team member ventures onto the other team's territory, he is at risk of being caught (tagged) by the enemy team. When caught he is taken to that team's jail, where he must remain until he is freed (touched) by one of his team members.

When someone manages to capture the other team's flag and return it to their own territory, their team wins. This is when it is time to bring out red, white, and blue Bomb Pops (found in your grocer's frozen food case) and celebrate both the win and the flag! As you lick the Bomb Pops and talk about the game's action, move the conversation toward recognizing the flag. With your displayed flag in view, salute it and pledge allegiance to it. You will see as the children in Wisconsin, New York, and Chicago did that having a party is still a good way to celebrate Flag Day.

⚜

While children got the idea of a Flag Day going, it needed presidents and congress to make it a *national* event. When President Wilson wanted the country to feel patriotic during World War I, a *national* flag day was organized. Recognizing our flag encourages patriotism.

When Americans felt proud because our soldiers helped win World War II, it was definitely time to fly the flag!

This flag history convinced Congress that it was time June 14 became a legal holiday, and President Truman signed the law into effect in 1949.

Having it as law, though, doesn't guarantee recognition. People need to respond in some way, and we can. We can keep the significance and power of our flag alive by displaying it on June 14, saluting it, pledging it, singing about it, and sometimes even having a party! We can fly our flags with praise to God for all that He has done!

CHAPTER 12

Father's Day

"Turn the hearts of the fathers to their children, and the
hearts of the children to their fathers" (Malachi 4:6).

*I*f there's a day to recognize mothers, then why not a day to honor
fathers? This question ran through Sonora Smart Dodd's mind
as she sat in a Mother's Day service in the early 1900s. The sermon
naturally was about mothers, and as the minister preached, she
thought about her father. He had been so strong and loving, caring
for her and her five siblings after her mother died giving birth. *Fathers
deserved recognition, too, just like mothers did. Why not have a Father's Day?*

Mrs. Dodd wasn't the only one who thought of the idea, but
hers seemed to have the most momentum. She saw the celebration
as being a church event, so she talked with her minister about her
idea. He approved the idea and helped her to get support from other
ministers, churches, and the local YMCA. Together they sponsored
the celebration. It was held at Mrs. Dodd's church on the third Sunday
in June 1910, her father's birth month.

Mrs. Dodd's efforts to honor fathers received newspaper coverage,
and the idea spread throughout the country. Soon people around the
United States were celebrating Father's Day year after year. In 1972,
President Richard Nixon signed a congressional resolution fixing
Father's Day as a permanent holiday to be observed every year on
the third Sunday of June.

Since then, sons and daughters across the United States honor
fathers by recognizing their contributions, acknowledging the

importance of their role and showing their appreciation. This is a day when we express our love, respect, and gratitude for fathers.

Celebration chatter

At our house, when we are planning to honor someone, we usually begin by asking, "What do you want to eat?" We know we are going to have the joy of sitting at the table together and pleasing the honoree with his favorite foods and good conversation.

Once the food is prepared and we are sitting at the table, we begin the meal by thanking God for the honoree and asking God to bless him. This blessing spills over and is enhanced with table talk.

How well do you know Dad? If children are at your table, ask questions such as How tall is Dad? How old is Dad? What is Dad's favorite color? What is his favorite food? (This may be obvious by what's on the table!) What's Dad's favorite song? Where does Dad work? What does Dad do at work? Where was Dad born? What's Dad's favorite sport? What's Dad's favorite Bible verse? What's your favorite thing to do with Dad? These questions often result in delightful responses—ones Dad will enjoy hearing.

What do you think of Dad? If you have mostly older children, teenagers, and young adults at your table, ask questions that are more reflective and evaluative.

• What has your father taught you about God?
• What did your father teach you about hard work?
• What was the best piece of advice your father ever gave you?
• What do you admire about your father?
• How are you similar to your father?

Ask one of these questions and have each person in the celebration circle respond or place a different question at each plate. Ask each person around the table to read and answer his question.

What good is Dad? Author Harriet Ziefert and illustrator Amanda Haley created a cute little book called *33 Uses for a Dad.*

Each page lists a use such as pet feeder, ATM machine, map reader, storyteller, timekeeper, hand-holder, taxi, alarm clock, etc. There's a correspondingly cute illustration to go with each use. You could have your children verbalize their list of "uses" for Dad. See how long you can keep this list going by moving from one person to another around the table. In the end, all, including Dad, will realize just how valuable he is!

Why do we love Dad? Ask persons in the celebration circle to say why they love Dad. Each should state why he or she loves Dad plus remembering why others in the circle love him as well. One person starts by saying, "I love Dad because he's _____." Fill in the blank with any phrase that comes to mind! The next person states what this person says plus adds her own reason. For example, the first child says, "I love Dad because he comes to my ball games." The next child then says, "I love Dad because he goes to our ball games and because he helps me with my spelling words." The next person repeats the process, but this time she must say both the preceding two phrases before adding another phrase. Keep taking turns around the circle until it becomes impossible to remember all of the things said about Dad. By the time this activity ends, Dad's going to really feel loved.

Who were some dads in the Bible? Here's a little quiz to play at the table which should generate some discussion about fathers. Ask players to circle the correct answer. Answers are found in an endnote.[1]

1. Who was the father of Cain, Abel, and Seth?

   Adam   *Noah*   *Abraham*

2. What father took his three sons and their wives to safety, during a world catastrophe?

   Adam   *Noah*   *Abraham*

3. What father was willing to sacrifice the son of his old age because he thought God wanted him to?

Abraham   *Isaac*   *Jacob*

4. What father was deceived by a son who wanted his blessing?

Abraham   *Isaac*   *Jacob*

5. What father had sons who sold one of their brothers into slavery?

Abraham   *Isaac*   *Jacob*

6. What father tried to kill his son's best friend?

Jacob   *Saul*   *David*

7. What father cried in anguish, "O my son Absalom, would God I had died for thee"?

Jacob   *Saul*   *David*

8. What father had two daughters married to the same man?

Jacob   *Laban*   *Saul*

9. What father, a ruler of the synagogue, had his daughter brought back to life by Jesus?

Jairus   *James*   *Zechariah*

10. What father was unable to speak, because of unbelief, until his son was born?

Jairus   *James*   *Zechariah*

A dessert of words

As the main course ends, and while dessert is being served or right after it is served, give cards to Dad. These can be thoughtfully purchased cards or ones you have made. As you know from the Mother's Day chapter, I'm partial to the homemade ones. Here are some card ideas.

- Cut out the picture of an athlete from a magazine. Over the athlete, paste a picture of the father you want to honor. Print these words along the bottom: *My Hero, My Dad* or *You're a Real Champion.*
- Make a very long paper necktie and write on it: *Here's the world's longest tie for the world's greatest Dad! Happy Father's Day.*
- On some card stock, draw or paste some pictures of four-leaf clovers. On the inside put this saying: "I'm just as lucky as I can be for the world's best Dad belongs to me!"
- Instead of a flat folded card, decorate a box. Write compliments or facts about Dad on slips of paper. Your family members could write such statements as "Dad is a good listener," "Dad keeps our car running," "Dad is a great cook," and "Dad is a good pitcher." Dad can read all these when you present the box to him, making him feel really good at the moment. But he can also set the box on his dresser, desk, or workbench, and take two or three out to read from time to time when he needs some encouragement.

Gifts with promise

Another important part of honoring anyone is giving him gifts. You want to find that special gift for Dad which is going to please him. Perhaps that would be a gift that comes with a promise.

Gifts with the promise that you will do something "for" Dad. In her book *Holiday Fun Year-Round,* Dian Thomas offers some clever gift ideas with coupons tucked inside.

- Give Dad a pair of white cotton garden gloves. Decorate them with textile paints. Fill with Dad's favorite treats and coupons such as "Good for Lawn Mowing," "Good for Weeding," and "Good for Trimming."[2]

- Cut a fish shape out of poster board or cardboard. "Decorate it with spinners, flies, swivels, etc. Write on the fish 'Good for One Day of Fishing.'"[3]
- "Place sponges, car wax, car air freshener, etc., in the middle of a chamois. Wrap it up and tie a ribbon at the top. Add a coupon that says, 'Good for One Free Car Wash and Wax.'"[4]

Gifts with promise that you will do something "with" Dad. Rather than doing something *for* Dad, he might prefer that you do something *with* him. This is what one father said when I asked him how he wanted to be honored on Father's Day. Here are some gift ideas he suggested.

- Take him to a shop or a show about something that he is interested in (auto show, antiques, home shows).
- Buy the tickets to a ball game and go together to see the game.
- Take him to an outdoor music festival or to a concert which features his kind of music.
- Go fishing together.
- Take him shopping for a camera, figure out how to use it together, and follow through by taking some pictures.
- Go camping together in a scenic area where they could do some night star gazing.

In summary, he said, "I would like activities that have to do with bonding." Spending time together builds and enriches a relationship. In the busyness of our lives, this is something we might not get around to doing, so perhaps Father's Day could be that time when we pledge to do something with Dad.

Widening your celebration circle

We refer to George Washington as the Father of Our Country, the men who helped form the United States as Founding Fathers, and Albert Einstein as the Father of Modern Science. In this way we recognize characteristics that go with fatherhood. These men were not our physical fathers, but they led, guided and taught—traits often associated with dads.

Keeping this thought in mind, you might want to widen your Father's Day celebration circle to include others beside your actual physical father. Your celebration might include granddads, fathers-in-law, uncles, stepfathers, mentors, coaches, and Sunday School teachers. You could honor men who are caring and supportive, men who have—or who are—making a difference in your life.

Father's Day nudges us into making an effort to thank these men. This could be a day when we honor those who are like fathers to us.

- Invite them to share your Father's Day meal.
- Write a note of thanks and appreciation, making sure you tell them how they have influenced your life.
- Invite them to do an activity with you and nurture the relationship.

Another way you might want to think about widening your Father's Day celebration circle is by including fathers who might be overlooked on this holiday. Honoring this kind of father wouldn't be because he's been a fatherlike person to you. Rather honoring would be a ministry.

- Invite a single father with young children to share the Sunday holiday with you. Invite him and his children to your worship service then to your house for a scrumptious meal and fellowship. If the children are young, have craft materials out where they can make Poppa a card while you are getting the food on the table.
- Invite a widowed father from your church, someone whose adult children live too far away to return home for the holiday. Father's Day is not a great "travel back home" holiday like Christmas is. You can add brightness to an otherwise lonely heart by sharing your celebration with him.
- Visit a home for older people in your community on Father's Day. Visit with the men in the hallways and dining room. Give them a card or a flower. Roses are traditional for Father's Day as

carnations are for Mother's Day.[5] Ask the fathers you meet to tell you about their children and if they have any advice for today's parents.

As we widen our celebration circle, we want to make sure we include the Father of all fathers. As we are thinking about the characteristics of human fathers on Father's Day, this gives us a prime opportunity to consider our heavenly Father's nature. As your group discusses what they admire about fathers, what they count on from their fathers, or what they appreciate about their fathers, perhaps they will increase their appreciation of God. If not, here's a matching exercise, they can do. Connect the *earthly* father trait with the *heavenly* Father trait mentioned in the Bible verses.

_____ 1. A father protects.

A. "Our fathers disciplined us for a little while as they thought best; but God disciplines us for our good, that we may share in his holiness" (Hebrews 12:10).

_____ 2. A father guides.

B. "If you . . . know how to give good gifts to your children, how much more will your Father in heaven give good gifts to those who ask him!" (Matthew 7:11).

_____ 3. A father loves.

C. "The son said to him, 'Father, I have sinned against heaven and against you. I am no longer worthy to be called your son.' But the father said to his servants . . . Let's . . . celebrate. For this son of mine was dead and is alive again; he was lost and is found'" (Luke 15:21–22, 24).

_____ 4. A father disciplines.

D. "As a father has compassion on his children, so the Lord has compassion on those who fear him" (Psalm 103:13).

_____ 5. A father forgives.

E. "I will lead them beside streams of water on a level path where they will not stumble, because I am Israel's father" (Jeremiah 31:9).

_____ 6. A father provides.

F. "Holy Father, protect them by the power of your name— the name you gave me—so that they may be one as we are one" (John 17:11).

_____ 7. A father cares.

G. "How great is the love the Father has lavished on us, that we should be called children of God! And that is what we are!" (1 John 3:1).

This quiz is not meant to imply that everyone's earthly father has all of these traits, but it does mean that God does. As His children, we experience these traits and learn these things are true about Him.

That's why we can't help but respond to Him with "Abba, Father!" And that's why when we pray, we say, "Our Father, who art in heaven." Whether we have a living earthly father, whether we have a supportive father figure in our lives, we have a heavenly Father who loves us, guides us, protects us, disciplines us, cares for us, and provides for us! That's reason enough to celebrate Father's Day!

Independence Day

*"Proclaim liberty through out the land to
all its inhabitants" (Leviticus 25:10).*

O h, Bob, come and look!" It was early in the morning of July 4.
I had stepped outside to put a couple of American flags in a
planter when I glanced up the hill toward our roadside mailbox. An
American flag was beside it! *Where did that come from*? The neighbors
across the road had one beside their mailbox too. Looking further,
I saw other flags up and down the road in our subdivision. What a
sight! This was something my husband had to see.

Where the flags came from we had no idea, but it was nice to
know someone else "out there" shared our patriotic spirit. Someone
else recognized the importance of celebrating Independence Day.
This day's name gives the reason why we celebrate on the Fourth
of July.

From dependence to independence

Back in the 1700s, before there was a United States of America, there
were 13 colonies that were ruled by Britain. The colonists had come
here hoping for a better life, and some even hoping to find freedom.
Many of them found what they were looking for. Their lives were
better as they made use of this country's natural resources but
they weren't free to solve what problems they did have. England
controlled them even though they were miles away, but there was

little response from Britain when there were problems. The colonists couldn't count on help from England even though they paid taxes to the king.

As taxes increased, the colonists became frustrated and angry. They felt they should get something back for what they paid; they should have a voice in determining how they were governed.

The colonist leaders met together and talked about their concerns. They determined they wanted change even if it meant fighting, which it did. The Revolutionary War began in 1775.

The colonists decided they needed a written declaration of their desire for freedom. They needed a document to explain why they wanted to be free from England. Their leaders worked on this document which stated that they refused to be subject to British leaders or laws. They wanted to choose their own leaders, govern themselves, and make their own laws. They signed this Declaration of Independence on July 4, 1976.

This date is considered the birth date of the United States of America, so on the Fourth of July, it's time to sing "Happy Birthday" to the USA. Bring out the cake, light the candles, and redeclare our independence.

- Have an older teen or an adult read out loud, in performance mode as if he were doing this on stage, the Declaration of Independence or portions of it. This can be very effective if your celebration involves a large group and is in a place where everyone can hear well. If your celebration includes small children, you might want to serve the birthday cake right before the reading begins.

- Use some words from the Declaration of Independence as a responsive reading, which is something we've frequently done in our family. I print the words on stiff white paper, roll the paper and tie with a red ribbon, and place one at each plate. Before my husband asks the blessing, we untie the document and read this together.

Bob: When in the Course of human events,

Brenda: it becomes necessary for one people to dissolve the political bands which have connected them with another,

Christophe: and to assume among the powers of the earth,

Bob: the separate and equal station to which the Laws of Nature and of Nature's God entitle them,

Ben: a decent respect to the opinions of mankind requires that they should declare the causes which impel them to the separation.

All: We hold these truths to be self-evident, that all men are created equal, that they are endowed by their Creator with certain unalienable Rights, that among these are Life, Liberty and the pursuit of happiness.

- For an even simpler, but still-makes-the-point activity, print the most famous sentence from the Declaration of Independence on table tents. Personalize the quote a little as I have done here: "We hold these truths to be self-evident, that all of us are created equal, that we are endowed by our Creator with certain unalienable Rights, that among these are Life, Liberty and the pursuit of Happiness." Ask family members and/or guests to read this quote out loud with you before the blessing. During the meal, if celebration chatter allows, ask, What do the words "unalienable Rights" mean? What does it mean that all Americans have the right to "Life, Liberty and the pursuit of Happiness?" What makes you happy?

Recognizing freedom

Redeclaring our independence is another way of saying we value liberty. This is something we may take for granted even as we enjoy life and pursue happiness. Perhaps calling some attention to liberty would help raise our appreciation level.

Find liberty. Print on separate pieces of paper several copies of each letter in the words *liberty, independence,* and *freedom*—three words that mean the power to act, speak, or think without externally imposed restraints. Hide the papers around the room. Divide the players into teams if you have a large group. (If not, let it be an individual activity.) Explain that each team is to find the letters to spell *liberty, independence,* and *freedom.* The team that finds all the letters and places them in the correct order first wins. While you have their attention, and as you're passing out sparklers to the winners, talk about what these words mean.

Ring liberty. The Liberty Bell, which hangs in Independence Hall in Philadelphia, is a treasured symbol of America's independence. This historic bell was rung in 1776 to let everyone know that the Declaration of Independence had been approved. The inscription on the Liberty Bell says in part: "Proclaim liberty throughout the land." Ring a bell when calling your guests to eat their barbecued ribs and baked beans. Say, "Let's proclaim our liberty. Let's praise God we are free."

Read liberty. Every coin minted in the United States bears, along with the bust of a past hero, these words: *Liberty* and *In God We Trust.* Place some coins on the tablecloth around your Fourth of July centerpiece. Ask the children to pick up the coins and read what's on them before the blessing is said. Say something like this, "Our forefathers chose these words, for they knew that gaining our freedom and keeping it was linked to God. Let's express gratitude to God today, thanking Him for our forefathers and asking Him to help us be a nation that continues to trust in Him."

Hunt liberty. As Christ followers, we know where real liberty lies, in being free from the bondage and power of sin. We also know that obedience to God enhances our life and our pursuit of happiness. Bring Bibles to the table, and have family members hunt for verses about freedom and liberty: Leviticus 25:10a, Psalm 119:44–45, John 8:32, Romans 8:21, 1 Corinthians 7:22, Galatians 5:1, and 1 Peter 2:16.

See which child finds the verse first. Ask him or her to read the verse out loud.

Sing liberty. The song "America" begins with "My country, 'tis of thee, sweet land of liberty." To take a lung full of air and push it out with words from this song will make your heart swell with pride and gratitude for living in the land of the free. In fact, singing songs that exalt God and country may be just the patriotic touch your Fourth of July gathering needs.

Of Thee I Sing

Many songs about our country applauds our freedom, expresses patriotism and reveals our faith.

- "America the Beautiful"
- "Mine Eyes Have Seen the Glory" ("Battle Hymn of the Republic")
- "The Star Spangled Banner"
- "America" ("My Country, 'Tis of Thee")
- "God Bless America"
- "God Bless the U.S.A."
- "Lift Every Voice and Sing"
- "God of Our Fathers"

To make sure you sing these songs with the gusto they deserve, provide copies of the words for your participants. After all, how many times have you started to sing "The Star-Spangled Banner" and found you could only remember part of the words?

Look for God in patriotic songs. Photocopy some of these songs. Distribute these among family members and give each one a highlighter. Ask them to find and to highlight as many references to God as they can find.

"See" from sea to shining sea. Katherine Lee Bates wrote "America the Beautiful" after standing on Pikes Peak, looking out over the Colorado landscape. She wrote about "spacious skies," "amber waves

of grain," "purple mountain majesties," and the "fruited plain." We live in a beautiful country. The first verse ends as a prayer, asking God to shed His grace on America. Cut out pictures of various historic or scenic areas of the United States. Glue them to cardboard. Cut each picture into pieces and place in an envelope. Make one for each guest. Let each person choose an envelope. On signal, they begin putting the puzzles together. The first to complete a puzzle is the winner. A natural conclusion to this activity would be to sing the last verse of "America the Beautiful" or the first verse of "How Great Thou Art."

To Thee we pray

When we look back at a historical event, it is always to assume that once a decision was made, that was it. The case was closed, but with the Declaration of Independence, it wasn't that simple. The war which started in 1775 went on until 1783.

Our freedom came at a price, something John Adams, one of the signers, could see was going to happen. He wrote to his wife, "I am well aware of the toil and blood and treasure that it will cost to maintain this Declaration, and support and defend these States. Yet through all the gloom I can see the rays of ravishing light and glory. I can see that the end is worth more than all the means."[1]

Thank God for the courageous leaders who wrote and defended the Declaration of Independence. To help your children understand this, talk with them about what it would take to declare independence. Ask them, What would it require if you wanted to declare yourself independent of this family? Would it take courage? Would it take resourcefulness? Hopefully, this activity will give them some appreciation for those 56 men who signed the Declaration of Independence.

Thank God for those who continue to preserve our freedom. Freedom is never guaranteed. To keep our country free, men and women have to fight and to give their lives so we can continue to exercise our options. Invite military personnel or a military family to share in your Fourth of July festivities. Celebrate Independence Day with those who keep us independent. Let them hear you offer a prayer for them.

Look for the good and praise it. In a time when we're apt to focus more on what is wrong with our country than on what is right, Independence Day is a good time to pause and to consider what is right with the United States. Make a list of those things with your family and turn the list into a prayer of thanks. You might want to follow this prayer with the Pledge of Allegiance to the flag.

Pray to the God who was there—and who is still with us! The Declaration of Independence contains four statements of faith showing that those who signed it were very much aware of their need for God's help. If they were going to truly gain independence, they needed Him.

1. "We hold these truths to be self-evident, that all men are created equal, that they are endowed by their Creator with certain unalienable Rights."

2. "Appealing to the Supreme Judge of the world for the rectitude of our intentions."

3. "With a firm reliance on the protection of divine Providence."

4. "And to assume among the powers of the earth, the separate and equal station to which the Laws of Nature and of Nature's God entitle them."

Base your prayer on these self-evident truths. Speak to God as the Creator, the Supreme Judge of the world, the divine Providence, and God of nature. See what naturally flows in the remainder of your prayer as you think of God in the light of one of these names.

Any of these prayers would make for a solemn act of devotion to God Almighty, something John Adams thought ought to occur in future celebrations of the Day of Deliverance. He also thought future celebrations would include parades, games, sports, and noise!

A great anniversary festival

In a letter to his wife, Abigail, the one where he mentioned the dangers ahead, John Adams also said he believed the Day of Deliverance would be most memorable. He wrote, "I . . . believe that it will be celebrated by succeeding generations, as the great anniversary festival. It ought to be commemorated, as the Day of Deliverance, by solemn acts of devotion to God Almighty. It ought to be solemnized with pomp and parade, with shows, games, sports, guns, bells, bonfires and illuminations, from the end of this continent to the other, from this time forward forevermore."[2]

This is exactly what has happened. Through the years, and even today, the things he mentioned are still a part of our Fourth of July celebrations, including the noise!

Bring out your noisemakers. Gather the kazoos, the bells, the drums, the whistles—whatever noisemakers you have around the house. Use them to "make a joyful noise" (Psalm 66:1 KJV) after you have displayed the flag and pledged allegiance to it.

Make tambourines and sing. Accompany the singing of patriotic songs with tambourines. To make some, put some uncooked macaroni or dry beans between two paper plates and staple the plates together. Decorate the tambourines with ribbons or crayon drawings, and let the noise begin.

Let the children stomp and pop. Save all the bubble wrap that comes in packages through out the year. On July 4, give children pieces of bubble wrap to lay on the sidewalk and stomp on. They'll love the popping sound. Be sure to enlist their help in picking up the bubble wrap afterward to put in a recycling bin. We can remind them, "We not only want to celebrate America, we want to save America!"

Participate in a parade. Attend a parade organized by your community and listen to the sounds of the marching bands, or organize your own parade. Gather the children of your neighborhood or church together. Make a parade banner on a large sheet of butcher paper or an old sheet. With red and blue markers, write *Thank God for Freedom* or *God Bless America* on the banner. Select two people to hold it and lead the parade. Have the other kids follow with decorated bicycles, tricycles, riding toys, and wagons. Let the little children not riding beat an old pan with a spoon or jiggle a bunch of metal measuring spoons for a tinkling sound. Give those children without a noisemaker small American flags to carry and to wave. As you march, watch for smiles from the sidelines. Your viewers will be sharing in your festive spirit.

Watch fireworks. Fireworks have long been a part of Independence Day celebrations. Maybe it is because their booming noise reminds people of the war that occurred to make our independence possible. Or maybe it is because the noise reflects our thumping hearts when we are able to see what John Adams called "rays of ravishing light and glory."[3]

∽

Americans celebrate Independence Day in different ways, but we are all celebrating the same thing. Every year on July 4 we honor the birth of our nation. This is when our spirit unites with others as we sing, pray, display our flags, and shout "God bless America."

Labor Day

"Whatever you do, do it all for the glory of God"
(1 Corinthians 10:31).

What's on your mind as Labor Day approaches? Do you smell hot dogs? Do you hear hamburgers sizzling on the grill? Observed on the first Monday in September, this holiday marks the end of summer for many people. It's associated with one last trip to the lake, one last barbecue, or one last picnic.

The ending of summer wasn't on the mind of labor leader Peter McGuire when he thought up the idea of Labor Day in 1882. This was at a time when work conditions weren't what they are today; and before McGuire's time, the conditions had been even bleaker. Great strides had been made when McGuire thought having a "day off" would be a good way to honor American workers. Congress agreed. In 1892, the first Monday in September was made a holiday.

Progress continued to be made, so work conditions have greatly improved over what they were in the late 1800s, but workers could still use some applause. We are all dependent on workers for the kind of lifestyle we enjoy; and besides, working pleases God. As we please Him with our laboring, He blesses us and we can bless others.

The workers in your life

Day after day, workers can go unnoticed. They are simply a part of life's landscape. They are "just there" providing services, keeping systems going, developing products, and cleaning up after us. Labor Day says, "Stop. Think about these people, acknowledge what they do, and show some appreciation."

Explore with your family the many kinds of workers whose lives impact yours. Think of community helpers such as firefighters, police officers, dog catchers, and government officials. Think of professionals that help us learn and keep us healthy such as teachers, school administrators, doctors, nurses, dentists, and nutritionists. Talk about workers who "serve" such as barbers, hair stylists, grocery clerks, mail carriers, school bus drivers, waiters, and trash collectors. There are also office workers, factory workers, construction workers, salesmen, farmers, computer technicians, and so on, to consider. As you can see, the list can go on and on.

- Make a game out of this exploration. Starting with the person on your right, go around the table with each person naming a particular kind of worker. See who can go the longest in naming workers.
- Make the exploration a pencil and paper game seeing who can make the longest list of occupations.
- Explore the varieties of jobs with an alphabet approach. A could be for airline pilot, B could be for barber, and so on. If you need help for Q, X, and Z, they could be quality control inspector, x-ray technician, and zookeeper!

Recognize the value of these roles by showing some appreciation. Labor Day was organized because McGuire thought workers needed some appreciation. They were given a day off from work and honored with a parade. People clapped and cheered as workers walked by. Now it is time for us, in our own way, to do some cheering.

- Have you thanked a workman lately? Have PayDay candy bars and/or rolls of Life Savers on hand. Ask your children to give a bar or a roll to a worker of their choosing. This could be a neighbor, a church member, a relative, or a family friend. Suggest they say to the recipient something like this, "Here's a little 'pay' for you. Thanks for your labor!" or "You make *life* better for others with your hard work." If the children are reluctant to say these words, print them on a label and attach to the candy.

- Have each family member write a thank-you note to a worker. Have pens and paper handy. You could hand deliver these on Labor Day or on Tuesday mail these notes of gratitude. Either way, your family's thank-you notes will bring joy to those whose work contributions may go unnoticed.

- Give God thanks for laborers with a prayer something like this: "Father, we are blessed to have so many workers helping us to enjoy life, pursue our dreams, keeping us safe, helping us learn, and helping to keep America strong. We thank You for them and for the work they do. We ask that You bless them on this Labor Day, that they would feel appreciated, and are able to return to work on Tuesday with renewed vigor."

All in the family

As we raise appreciation for workers in general, we can also raise awareness for and increase appreciation for the workers in our own family with some around-the-table activities and conversation.

Work symbols. Have each family member identify a symbol of the work he or she does and bring it to the table. Even children work—or are supposed to!—so each can bring something that in his or her own eyes represents what he or she does. Examples of work for children include picking up toys, cleaning off the dinner table, feeding the dog, going to school, doing homework, etc. During the meal, ask each person to show his symbol and explain its connection with what he or she does.

Work questions. Throw out some questions as conversation topics when you eat together on Labor Day.

- Ask, What would happen if Dad or Mom could not go to work anymore?
- Ask, Who doesn't quit working even on Labor Day when it is a holiday for workers? Who doesn't get a day off? (Three things you might want to point out in this conversation: [1] some jobs are ongoing, that have to be done even when there is a holiday; [2] some people still have to go to work on a day that is a holiday for workers; and [3] God never rests from doing His work of being God.)
- Ask your children, What do you want to be when you grow up? Or what do you want to do after high school? Let this conversation prompt them to think about the work they will want to do "someday."

Work incentive. Talk about the importance of "laboring" together to keep your household functioning. Discuss how it takes everyone working together. You might want to call their attention to 2 Thessalonians 3:10 (GNT): "Whoever refuses to work is not allowed to eat." These words would make a great quote for your kitchen wall or to post on your refrigerator!

Parental work. Explain what you and your spouse do when you are at your jobs away from home. Some children have no concept of what their parents do when they're at work. What do you actually do? Do you sit or stand? Do you run a machine? Do you have to wear special clothing? Around the table on Labor Day fill your family in what your workdays look like. Help them visualize what you do and what blessings God gives your family through your work.

Conclude your table exercises and discussion with prayer for each other. Children pray for parents. Parents pray for children. Labor Day may be a time of transition for children from summer play to being in school. Pray for them to adjust, to be eager to learn, to be earnest workers, and to appreciate their teachers.

Labor Day

The biblical view

Sometime on Labor Day morning give family members a *work* sheet. If they complain, ask them to remember that this is *Labor* Day. Also tell them you'll have a nice prize waiting for the first one to complete the quiz and for the one having the most right answers. Many workers need to be motivated! Ask them to use their Bibles to find answers to the following questions.

- The first verb in the Bible is a working verb. What is it? (Genesis 1:1)
- Who was doing the work of creating? (Genesis 1:1)
- What did God think of His work? (Genesis 1:31)
- What work did God give man and woman to do? (Genesis 2:15)
- What did God curse that makes work harder for many people? (Genesis 3:17).
- How much of our time is to be spent working? (Exodus 20:9)
- Who worked really hard so that she and her mother-in-law, both widows, could survive? (Ruth 2:2, 7)
- What work did Ruth do? (Ruth 2:2, 7)
- What will the worker of the land be blessed with? (Proverbs 12:11; 28:19)
- What's the reward of hard work and of mere talk? How are they different? (Proverbs 14:23)
- What insect gives us a good example for working? (Proverbs 6:6–8)
- Who should take a lesson from ants? (Proverbs 6:6–8)
- What's one thing we can learn from ants? (Proverbs 6:6–8)
- How long does a good woman work? (Proverbs 31:18, 27)
- What kind of effort is to be put into working? (Ecclesiastes 9:10)
- What harsh words did Jesus have for the man who did not work to increase his talent? (Matthew 20:1–15)
- What was Jesus' occupation? (Mark 6:3)
- What did Jesus say about His work the night before He died? (John 17:4)

- What kind of work did Paul encourage the Thessalonians to do? (1 Thessalonians 4:11)
- Why should we make this kind of work our ambition? (1 Thessalonians 4:12)
- Whose work example did Paul say the Christians should follow? (2 Thessalonians 3:7-8)
- Why did Paul work so hard? (2 Thessalonians 3:8–9)
- Or what did Paul want to show others by his hard work? (2 Thessalonians 3: 9)
- What rule about working did Paul give the Christians at Thessalonica? (2 Thessalonians 3:10b)
- What did Paul encourage busy bodies and idle people to do? (2 Thessalonians 3:11–12)
- How long should we work at doing right? (2 Thessalonians 3:13).

By the number of questions here, you can see how much the Bible has to say regarding work. Would you believe I could have included even more references?

As it is, this quiz may be too long for a holiday activity, but feel free to pick and choose questions appropriate for your family members, their ages, and the time you have.

You could use a quiz about work as a morning breakfast activity, in that lazy hour following a holiday breakfast before everyone gets active, or in the car on the way to a family gathering.

To do this quiz is to search the Scriptures about work. What the Bible says encourages the development of a work attitude and ethic that pleases God. Almost everyone gets disgruntled with work at some time or other because work requires effort and self-discipline. The quiz's answers remind us of some important truths that should help keep us motivated.

- Work is not a curse. From the beginning God meant for us to work.
- Work makes up the greater portion of our waking hours.
- Work is the way we take care of ourselves and our families.

- Work provides us with a purpose and helps us be productive.
- The way we work serves as an example to others.
- The way we work determines how much we appreciate working. Our attitude makes a difference.
- Work destroys idleness, and idleness can cause trouble.
- Our work gives God a chance to bless us and provide for us.
- Our work gives us an opportunity to bless others.

But as meaningful as our work is, as good as it makes us feel to be employed and/or to be productive, we also need times to rest. This is also a part of the Labor Day celebration and also a part of God's plan.

The last summer holiday

Many Americans like to get together with family and friends in their backyards or at a park somewhere on Labor Day. They feel with school being in full throttle and the busyness of fall coming on that it is their last chance for relaxing out-of-doors. So how can a spiritual emphasis still be put in a holiday like this?

Rest. Breathe. Enjoy. While God purposefully wants us to work, and to be diligent workers, God also wants us to be refreshed through resting. Realizing "this is the day that the Lord hath made," take in the refreshment that the out-of-doors offers, look around at His creative handiwork, praise Him, and enjoy your time fellowshipping with each other.

Have a parade. On the first Labor Day, there was a big parade in New York City, and many communities still have parades. But if you are away from your community, you might organize a parade at your picnic site. Gather the children and give them different work tools to carry in the parade: a hoe, a broom, a mop, a shovel, a hammer, etc. Have them march around the picnic area singing, "To the work! To the work! We are servants of God, let us follow the path that our Master has trod."[1]

Have a job search about 30 minutes before blessing the meal. Give children a piece of paper and ask them to mingle among the guests to find as many different kinds of workers as they can. Or ahead of time, if you know specifically who is coming, list the various jobs on paper. Have the children to find a worker for each listed job and get the person's autograph. As you go over the names when the sheets are returned, say a few words of appreciation for the workers. Then as you thank God for the food, also thank Him for the workers who are present.

Make your picnic a ministry. Invite those you know who are out of work and needing a job to share in your Labor Day cookout. The cheerful gathering, the delicious food and the fellowship will do much to encourage them as they pursue a job. By including them, you'll capture the essence of Jesus' story about ministering to others in His name (see Matthew 25:31–46).

Make the most of the moment even if ants show up, as they sometimes do. Turn their presence into a lesson. The Bible does. It insists you can learn from the ants' ways and be wise. "For though they have no [boss] to make them work, yet they labor hard" (Proverbs 6:7–8 TLB).

All around us are various ways we can connect with God when we are outdoors if we will but notice them, and we can when we are resting and relaxing. We can give our minds over to other things besides work when we enjoy a day off in a place where we can see God's handiwork. And on Tuesday, we'll be ready to return to our workplaces. And because we're refreshed and renewed, we can "give" ourselves "fully to the work of the Lord, because" we "know that" our "labor . . . is not in vain" (1 Corinthians 15:58).

Columbus Day

"Listen O isles, unto me; and hearken, ye people,
from afar; the Lord hath called me" (Isaiah 49:1 KJV).

In 1492, Christopher Columbus sailed the ocean. Today, hundreds of years later, we remember him on the second Monday of each October. Why? Who was he? What did he do? And why do Americans consider him important enough to have a holiday to honor him?

Columbus, a visionary

Christopher Columbus was born in 1451 in Genoa, Italy. His father was a weaver, and as a child, Columbus helped him make cloth. His heart wasn't in it, though. What he really wanted to do was be a sailor.

His father knew Columbus dreamed about sailing the seas, so when he was a teenager, his father asked him to sell their cloth in faraway places. Columbus jumped at the chance. As he traveled by boat from place to place, he gained valuable experience including how to sail large ships and use navigational instruments.

Later he worked with his brother as a mapmaker. He became adept at reading charts and analyzing maps. As his knowledge increased and he became an experienced sailor, an idea started taking shape in his mind. He dreamed of a new route to reach Asia (Japan, China, India, and the East Indies). The usual route was to travel *east* from Europe, which was a really long and hard trip. You had to sail south and then east around Africa.

But Columbus was the kind of person who wasn't afraid to ask, "Why not another way? What else is possible?" He studied, thought, and prayed. He concluded that you could get to Asia—and he thought more quickly—by traveling *west* from Europe.

As the idea solidified and took shape, he started talking about it. As he discussed the possibility of a shorter and faster route to Asia, some sailors were convinced. They thought Columbus's idea could work, but others didn't. What do you think?

Using a globe as your centerpiece for your Columbus Day meal or a world map displayed nearby, ask your tablemates to locate Columbus's starting point (Spain) and to locate Japan. Which way looks the shortest? To travel *east* from Spain or travel *west* to reach Japan? Why couldn't Columbus see what we can see? Explain that the maps he studied didn't show North and South America and the Pacific Ocean lying between him and Asia. No one knew about the Americas.

From the information he had, Columbus was confident of a better route, but he needed help to test his theory. Reaching Asia by an alternate route would be dangerous and expensive which is why he ended up leaving from Spain and not Italy.

Gaining support, being prepared

Columbus didn't have the resources to pay for a voyage of thousands of miles. Buying just one ship was extremely expensive and, for safety, he really needed two or three. He needed a crew to run the ships; and the crew members had to be paid and fed.

Columbus tried to persuade rich people to help him. He went to the kings and queens of various European countries trying to get them to back a trip to Asia by a new route. He reminded them of how discovering a shorter route would be beneficial, of the glory they would receive from this new endeavor, and the bounty he might be able to bring back. Asia was *the* place for valuable commodities such as spices, silk, medicines, scents, gold, and precious stones.

Some said, "A trip like this would cost way too much." Others said, "Sailing west to Asia will never work." Most considered a trip like this a waste of time and money. Among those who said no to his proposition were King Ferdinand and Queen Isabella of Spain. This was in 1486.

Even with all the rejections, Columbus never gave up his dream. He was convinced he was right plus he was confident God was leading him. He believed that God wanted him to take Christianity to other places. His first name, Christopher, which means "Christ bearer," was to him a clear indication that God's hand was directing him so he pressed on. He again approached the king and queen of Spain early in 1492. This time, Queen Isabella agreed to pay for his voyage. She gave him what he needed: a crew, food, money, and three ships.

Columbus's experience in gaining support is a reminder that all believers need to be prepared to "go" (Matthew 28:19–20; Acts 1:8). We always need to be thinking about where to go, how we will get there, what we will need for travel, how we will provide for ourselves, and what resources our work will require. And if we don't "go," we need to think about how we can help those who do.

- Raise awareness about preparedness by doing this fun activity using the ABC's. The first person starts with saying, "I'm going to Argentina, and I'm going to take Apples with me." The second person says, "I'm going to Belize, and I'm going to take Bottles of water and Apples with me." The third persons says, "I'm going to Columbia, and I'm going to take Carrots, Bottles of water, and Apples." See who can go the longest repeating all the items in alphabetical order. The last one remaining is the winner!
- Have children make replicas of the three ships that transported Columbus and his crew to "Asia." The three ships were the *Niña*, the *Pinta*, and the *Santa Maria*. Use the ships as places to deposit money and written prayers to support a mission or to take a missions trip. Make sure you have some slips of paper and pencils near the ships for writing brief prayers.

The voyage west

Like other vessels of that time, the *Niña,* the *Pinta,* and the *Santa Maria* were made of wood and powered by the wind trapped in their sails. It took strength and experience to raise and lower the heavy sails. The ships were crowded, cold, damp, smelly, and infested with fleas and rats. The ships leaked and had to be pumped out every day. The food was bad, and the sea was rough. There were no beds so the sailors slept anywhere they could find some space during their four-hour rest periods. They worked four hours and then rested four, then back to work for four. This left them feeling tired most of the time and many got sick. Frustrated and angry, they criticized Columbus.

Fueling their frustration was the fact that the trip got longer and longer. Columbus had figured the trip to Japan was about 2,734 miles away, but it was 9,320 miles further! The men had never sailed so long without seeing land.

As the voyage dragged on, with no sighting of Asia, the crew wondered if they were doomed to die. On October 10, 1492, the crew of the *Santa Maria* said to Columbus, "This voyage has gone on long enough. Turn the ship around; let's go home."

Columbus understood their frustration; he was getting weary himself, but he couldn't bring himself to give up. Columbus prayed about what to do. Then he said to the crew, "Give me three more days." As the third day begin to dawn, they spotted items that indicated they were near land. Hours later on October 12, 1492, they landed on an island in the Bahamas. With that landing, a whole New World opened up.

We know these things about Columbus's voyage even though it happened many years ago because he kept detailed journals— something we can do to celebrate Columbus Day and enrich our lives at the same time.

Start a family journal. Buy a large spiral notebook and paste a picture of your family on the front. On Columbus Day, have it accessible where everyone can conveniently write a line or two about your family: where you live, how old everyone is, what your family life is like, and what your goals are for the future. Every Columbus Day, bring out the journal, read previous entries, and write new ones. You'll discover and appreciate the journey your family is on. It won't have the same dynamics as Columbus's, but every family's journey is significant and worth recording.

Start individual journals. On Columbus Day, give each family member a journal. Encourage them to start keeping an account of their life, particularly their dreams and goals, what they are studying and learning, the places they would like to visit, missions goals they would like to accomplish, and meaningful Bible verses. Each Columbus Day, ask them to bring their journals to the table and read something they recorded in the last year.

Create a Christ bearer's journal. We are all to be Christ bearers even if our name isn't Christopher. God calls us all to share Christ and explore new-to-us territories. We can nurture this spirit in our family members—and honor Columbus at the same time—by keeping a specific journal about missions possibilities. Have family members record their answers to questions like these: If God called me to be an explorer like Columbus, where would I like to go? What missions area would I most like to visit and why? What would I want to do there? How would I treat the people I meet? How would I travel? By boat? Plane? Bicycle? Camel? Motorcycle? What do I need to do to prepare?

Dream fulfilled, or was it?

When Columbus landed on that first island in the Bahamas, he thought he had reached Asia, but yet he was perplexed. The people who lived there were friendly but they looked so different from what he expected. He scratched his head, *If this is Asia, why aren't people wearing silk robes? Where are the jewels I've heard so much about? Where are the palaces roofed in gold?*

There was some gold present, though. Some of the indigenous people were wearing gold necklaces. To Columbus, this meant there had to be gold nearby! He was determined to find it, moving beyond the first island and traveling to other places. He forced local men to guide his ships to find the gold. Before this, Columbus seemed intent on spreading Christianity, finding a better route to Asia, and helping Spain; but now, the desire for gold seemed to drive him forward.

Besides making local people help him find gold, Columbus took some of them back to Spain where he received a hero's welcome. The king and queen were impressed with what he had done. They eagerly agreed to pay for another voyage. They hoped he'd conquer more land, convert people to Christianity, and find more gold!

Still thinking he had reached Asia, Columbus returned to the area and continued to explore. All together Columbus made four voyages across the Atlantic Ocean. He visited the present-day countries of Cuba, Haiti, the Dominican Republic, Jamaica, Puerto Rico, and Panama, and even a portion of South America. The glory, though, faded when Columbus was accused of misconduct and was sent home to Spain in disgrace. But he returned on yet another voyage. This time he and his crew got stranded on a sandbank in Panama and then were marooned on Jamaica for a year.

Columbus eventually returned to Spain as a tired, ill, bitter, angry, and deeply discouraged man. His explorations had exhausted him. He died in Spain in 1506. When Columbus died, he had almost been forgotten by people, and he was out of favor with the queen. He had no idea that hundreds of years later people would honor him—a man who had missed his mark. He didn't find a shortcut to Asia, but he opened up a New World.

Those areas that Columbus discovered were unknown to Europeans; they didn't even know such places existed. After Columbus's explorations, they came and settled in these places. Columbus's voyages changed their view of the world.

To appreciate why this man whose actions weren't always perfect is honored, play a "what if" game. Around the table, discuss these questions.

- *What if* Christopher Columbus hadn't learned how to sail?
- *What if* Christopher Columbus hadn't become a mapmaker?
- *What if* Christopher Columbus had given up hope in seeking support?
- *What if* Christopher Columbus hadn't followed his dream?
- *What if* Christopher Columbus hadn't listened to God?
- *What if* he hadn't searched for gold?

His desire to find gold seemed at times to overtake reason, but yet his explorations opened a New World—a world that included the United States.

Hero come lately

After the United States was formed in 1776, people took interest in the nation's roots. They wondered, *How did this land open up to us?* Consequently, on October 12, 1792, some people in New York City honored the 300th anniversary of Columbus's landing in the Americas. You might say this was the first Columbus Day!

One hundred years later, on the 400th anniversary of Columbus's landing, people across the United States celebrated again. Yearly Columbus Day celebrations were begun 28 years later, even though it was still not a legal national holiday. Congress made it one in 1971. They also decided that Columbus Day would be held on the second Monday in October, giving people a three-day weekend.

Making it a national day of remembrance doesn't mean that everyone chooses to celebrate Columbus Day in the same way.

- Some people do applaud Columbus with parades and festivities.
- Some Italian Americans celebrate their Italian heritage and culture on this holiday. They connect with Columbus because he was Italian.

- Others prefer to honor the people he mistreated, the people who were already living in the Caribbean when he arrived. He called them Indians because he thought he had landed in India. The more preferable label now—and rightly so—is Native American.

Whether we are Native American, Italian American, or some other kind of American, we can celebrate by being explorers like Columbus. We don't have to sail the ocean blue; we can explore what's in our area and get to know the people around us. Our exploration may open up a whole "new world" of recognition.

Who was here first? Ask your celebration group to answer the question, Who was here before we got here? This could be in a general sense: Who was in the Caribbean when Columbus arrived? Who was in what is now the United States at that time? Or you could explore who was here first in a more specific sense. Who was in your town first? Who founded the community? Why was it started? Whether you take a general or specific approach, ask, "How has their being here first influenced life as it is today? How may we show our appreciation?"

Who's around us? As a family or a group, make a list of the various kinds of people in your area. These may not initially come to mind because they have simply become a part of the landscape. This happens as we unconsciously follow the same paths day after day and mingle with the same people over and over. You may even want to take a drive and visit different areas of the community. If there is no school, this would be a good Columbus Day activity. Give your children small tablets in which to keep a log or to jot down observations. Encourage them to talk to people and to take pictures. Ask them to report their findings at your evening meal. Then ask, "What do we have or enjoy because of them?" Conclude the discussion with a prayer of gratitude.

One thing that might alert you to the presence of different groups in your area is food. By our food, we are known! With our food, we celebrate!

Around the table

The various approaches to observing Columbus Day can be brought together into one celebration with food. With a four-course meal at home or with a progressive dinner at four different places, you can honor Columbus, recognize Native Americans, and spotlight Italian culture.

First course. Start the meal with something Spanish, representing the country that supported Columbus. Since this would begin the meal, make it something light and simple. At our house, a warm tortilla with a little butter or some cheese would be a perfect starter.

Second course. This would feature the food Columbus and his crew members would have eaten: salted meats, sardines, olives, peas, cheese, and raisins. Crew members often ate only one meal a day and they ate with their hands! Your children should like this!

Third course. Columbus and his crew encountered foods new to them when they arrived in the Caribbean. They ate what the indigenous people ate: yams, peppers and chilies, maize (yellow corn), kidney beans, and fruit. One source said the natives ate roasted iguana, but I don't recommend your making this a part of your Columbus Day celebration!

Fourth course. End the meal with Italian food such as spaghetti or some other pasta dish. If you think everyone will be full by the time they get to this last course (they really liked those sardines and yams!), just top off the evening with some spumoni (Italian ice cream).

At each course, engage your group in conversation about Columbus's dream and exploration, about those who helped support his dream, about the Native Americans who welcomed and fed Columbus and his crew, and for aspects of Italian culture that we all enjoy. Conclude the meal with a prayer of appreciation and gratitude. Here's one you might want to use. It's the author's paraphrase of part of a Native American prayer.

"Today we have gathered because we have been given the duty to live in balance and harmony with each other. So now, we unite our minds and hearts together and give thanks to You, God, our Creator."

Halloween

"Since you have become the Lord's people,
you are in the light. So . . . live like people
who belong to the light" (Ephesians 5:8 GNT).

H alloween, a popular holiday in the United States, is observed every October 31 with many different symbols and activities. Someone arriving here from outer space and seeing witches, devils, fairy princesses, tombstones, parties, pranks, and spider webs might scratch his head trying to figure out the meaning. Sometimes I do too! Just what is Halloween all about?

When I asked a ten-year-old, he said "Candy!" Yes, Halloween has come to be about candy too. Everyone wants some! Six-foot trick-or-treaters are prompting some communities to put an age limit on how old you can be to trick-or-treat.

With so many features, Halloween does not seem to have a clear, specific purpose. At least one I could find! Its beginnings—and notice that is plural—date back hundreds of years, and then through history other customs were attached making it the conglomerate that it is today.

Many Christians choose not to celebrate this holiday because many of the older practices come from pagan practices and are associated with evil and darkness. Richard Foster, the author of *Celebration of Discipline,* questions this. He writes, "Why allow Halloween to be a pagan holiday in commemoration of the powers of darkness? Fill the house or church with light: sing and celebrate the victory of Christ over darkness."[1] This is the approach we are going to take. To put the holy into this holiday, we're going to shine some light.

Let your pumpkin light shine

Years ago, a friend gave me a ceramic pumpkin with open spaces for the face's features. Every year it is a joy to get it out, put a candle in it, light it, and let its smile generate goodwill to all who see it. What would a lighted pumpkin say at your house?

Express happiness of sadness? Work together as a family to carve a happy face in one pumpkin and a sad face in the other. Put candles in each. Turn out the lights. Contrast the happy pumpkin face and the sad one. Decide together which is the best face. Talk about how faces represent inner feelings. Mention how our smiles and laughter can bring joy to others.

Radiate individuality? Purchase a pumpkin for each member of your family—a tiny one for your toddler, a medium-size one for your preteen, a tall oval one for Dad, etc. Have each person carve a face that represents him or her. As you complete this activity together, place candles in the pumpkins. Talk about the individuality of the pumpkins and about how each of us, in our own way, can let our light shine. Sing together "This Little Light of Mine."

Reflects Jesus? Put a large candle in a carved or ceramic pumpkin. Darken the room. Watch the flame as it fills the pumpkin and lights the room. As the light of the pumpkin illuminates the room, talk about how Jesus is the Light of the world (John 8:12 and 9:5) and can penetrate darkness. Sing together "Shine, Jesus Shine."

Shining light on salvation

Among all of Halloween's symbols, the pumpkin to me was always a safe Halloween symbol for Christians to celebrate with. You couldn't connect it with a pagan source. God made the pumpkin! Its use, though, as a jack-o'-lantern can be traced to an old Irish fable involving an evil man. Jack was so evil that neither heaven nor hell wanted him. All he could do was wander around in the dark.

Eventually, the devil felt sorry for Jack and gave Jack a glowing coal. With this light, he could see where he was going. The coal, though, was too hot to hold, so he carved a turnip and stuck it inside. This became his lantern, and it became known as a jack-o'-lantern as in "Jack of the lantern."

Others imitated Jack's practice as they lived in fear of the many evil spirits "out there" in the darkness. They hollowed out squash, turnips, and rutabagas. Grotesque faces were carved in the vegetables. Lighted candles were placed inside to light up the ugly faces, fend off the darkness, and to scare away evil spirits on Halloween, the night when their activity would be greatest.

When thousands of Irish came to the United States in the 1840s, they brought this Halloween practice with them. Once here, they discovered that it was much easier to carve a pumpkin than to carve a turnip! Pumpkins were plentiful in America, and they became popular as jack-o'-lanterns.

- Tell the fable about Jack's story as your family makes a jack-o'-lantern together. Then ask and discuss questions such as these: What does it take to get into heaven? Is anyone so awful that he can't get in? How is a person saved from hell?
- Use the "surgery" of carving as an object lesson. Making a jack-o'-lantern means cutting it open, sticking your hand down inside, bringing out the "gook," the innards of the pumpkin, so the inside is clean and ready to hold a candle. All of us have "gook" inside us. The Bible makes this clear in Romans 3:23 (KJV): "All have sinned and come short of the glory of God." The Bible also makes it clear that we can be forgiven of these sins and be assured of a place in heaven. With this explanation, you can shine a light on salvation.

Spotlighting saints

Halloween gets its name because of when it occurs. It falls on the eve of a day to recognize saints. In the A.D. 700s, the church decided that November 1 would be named All Saints Day, or All Hallows (Holy Ones) Day. It was a time set aside to remember and honor special people who had died.

Naturally, the evening before All Hallows Day became known as All Hallows Eve, or Halloween. This timing reminds us that we have a rich heritage of faith that we can celebrate by looking at examples of lives dedicated to God.

Remember saints in your church who have died and gone to heaven. Our working definition of a *saint* for this exercise is the New Testament one: Someone who believes in Jesus and has dedicated his life to serving the Lord. I was at a church last Halloween where this was very well done. The pictures of those saints who had died in the last year were flashed one by one on a large screen. It was very moving, and I didn't even know the people!

Remember historical saints, celebrate their lives, learn from them, and be inspired. Some churches will have official lists of saints, but most of us will be on our own. On my list, I would have Charles Wesley, John Wesley, Lottie Moon, Corrie ten Boom, Saint Francis of Assisi, William Carey, B. H. Carroll, William Barclay, and Martin Luther. Luther is someone we should definitely honor as a saint because it was on Halloween that he nailed his 95 theses on the door of Castle Church in Wittenberg, Germany, to usher in the Protestant Reformation. As a result, October 31 is also known as Reformation Day!

- Put the names of saints your family members might know—or need to know—in a basket. Have them draw a name and look up information about their saint at your library or online. Have them report back what they found when you eat together on Halloween. Better yet, since it is Halloween, have the person come to the table dressed as his saint. It doesn't have to be a complete costume, just something that would represent who the person is, enough for others to be able to recognize the saint.

- Ask each person at the table to write on a large sticky note the name of a saint. They make the determination instead of you! Collect the sticky notes in a basket. Pass the basket around and have all participants take out a sticky note and put it on another person's forehead for everyone to see, except for the person whose forehead it's stuck to. As you converse, participants try to guess whose saint they have on their forehead. The first person to guess who he is should get some reward. How about some extra Halloween candy!

Highlighting harvest

When these saint-honoring festivals were first held, they were held on May 13. The festivals became so popular, the crowds so large, that food was in short supply. This is why the feast was moved to November 1. The fall harvest provided an abundant food supply, and it still does. This makes Halloween a time ripe for celebrating God's goodness. We can praise Him for His creative work and thank Him for His provisions.

Take a trip to a pumpkin farm or a country market. Soak up fall's bounty and acknowledge God's goodness. Point out the squash, turnips, cornstalks, pears, and apples. Remind your celebration group that not everyone has harvest items like these. We who live in the United States are blessed with an abundance of food. We have much to be thankful for. Sing "God Is So Good" and offer sentence prayers on the way home in the car.

Have a harvest party outside, of course, in the late afternoon. "Gather" the harvest by having teams go from house to house, or in a general area, to collect items representative of fall. Be sure to set a time limit and a neighborhood boundary line. Hopefully, they will return with autumn flowers, pinecones, cornstalks, assorted leaves, and nuts. As darkness begins to fall, have the guests roast hot dogs and marshmallows over an open fire. After eating, while still sitting around the fire, sing songs and tell stories. End the party with devotional thoughts about the beauty of God's creation and a prayer of thanks for His goodness.

Lighting a fire

Bonfires, like the one mentioned in the harvest party above, were once a part of Halloween activities. Early on, more than 2,000 years ago, October 31 was the last day of the *year* for the Celts who lived in Great Britain, Ireland, and northern France. They called this day Samhain [SOW-in], which means "summer's end." They believed that the separation between the spirit and physical world was weakest on the last night of the year, allowing evil spirits to roam the earth. They lit fires, and let them burn bright, hoping the light would frighten the spooks away and prevent them from coming near. At the same time, they also wanted to attract good spirits. They welcomed them to their celebration hoping the good spirits would protect their homes in the coming year. Let's see what good we can do with a fire.

Build a bonfire at your Halloween gathering. Let it warm people's hearts as it warms people from the cold. Tell stories of the supernatural at work. Distinguish between the work of evil spirits and the work of the Holy Spirit. I used to tell my kids when they would go out to trick-or-treat, "Remember you don't believe in ghosts; you believe in the Holy Ghost (KJV word for Spirit)." Kids need to have an appreciation for the supernatural at work in their lives because of the spiritual nature of our faith.

Welcome trick-or-treaters with a fire in your front yard. OK, we're not talking bonfire here, but we are talking about light. A fire pit, for example, will draw people, who accompany their children. This will give you an opportunity to get to know your neighbors and other people. I read an account of one man who helped build his church this way. Because he was sitting outside in a lawn chair, with extra chairs for guests, people naturally gravitated toward him. They sat down for a while, conversation followed, and relationships were formed.

Shining light on who we really are

Children—and many adults too—like Halloween because it gives them an excuse to dress up as someone they are not. Never mind that the ancients wore masks to confuse evil spirits and to protect themselves. Your masquerading doesn't have to be for this reason. In my study of holidays, many cultures have donned costumes for various celebrations. It almost seems to be a part of our DNA to want to step outside of ourselves and briefly don another personality. Doing so fuels the imagination of children plus it is just plain fun for many people.

Have a "when the saints go marching in" party. Ask guests to come dressed as saints from Christian history. Have each saint announced when he or she enters the room. When everyone has gathered, march around the room with "When the Saints Go Marching In" playing in the background. *Or* instead of announcing who the saint is, you might want your party participants to guess who the "saints" are and who is impersonating the saint. If so, pin a large number on each costumed person as he or she arrives. Give each person a clipboard, and ask each to write down who the portrayed character (saint) is, and who the impersonator is. Give prizes for the best costumes, to the one who identifies the most saints, and to the person who identifies the most impersonators.

Have a "be a Bible character" party using the same kind of guessing approach. A Bible character party would offer a very wide range of "dress-up" possibilities from Roman soldiers to fishermen to kings and queens. Some teens and adults like to get into gore at Halloween. This is something else I don't understand—and wouldn't encourage—but if you have someone like that at your house, how about long-haired Samson carrying around the jawbone of a donkey (Judges 15:16)? Or Herod with John the Baptist's head on a plate (Mark 6:14–29)? At least, Bible research would be needed! And that is a good thing.

In either case—with historical saints or Bible characters—end your costume party with some thoughts on being authentic. Man looks on the outward appearance—the face we may show to the world—but God looks on the heart (1 Samuel 16:7). Our actions are to match what is in our hearts (1 John 3:18; Matthew 5:21 to 6:18). We are not to be hypocrites. We aren't to wear masks in our day-to-day lives. We are to be whom God created us to be, and one of the things He created us to do is to care about others.

Lighting up the lives of others

In medieval times, children wearing masks went from door to door "souling." They begged for "soul cakes," which were flat, oval shortbread cookies containing currants and various spices. If no soul cakes were forthcoming, the children played tricks or pranks on the guilty parties. As children of the light, called to spread the light, let's think of how we could brighten the lives of others without expecting anything in return.

- Treat others with the story of Jesus. Give out tracts that explain the plan of salvation to those who come trick-or-treating to your house. One woman I read about put a tract and a chocolate bar in a clear, resealable sandwich bag so they would stay together, and gave a bag to every trick-or-treater.
- Share your produce, the harvest from your garden, with others. Don't be stingy like Jack of jack-o'-lantern fame, which was his biggest crime. Donate your produce to a local food pantry.
- Make your own version of soul cakes (perhaps oatmeal cookies with raisins) and give them to local firefighters and police officers.

- Treat residents of a nursing home with soft pumpkin cookies. When your cookies are ready, contact the volunteer coordinator at the residency to determine the best time for dropping off your gifts.
- Give and greet. To satisfy that urge to dress up, have family members don costumes and add some brightness to the lives of others. Visit adults you know who are homebound. Let them have the fun of guessing who you are.

While the holiday of Halloween is a mixture of activities and symbols without a specific purpose, we can give use it purposefully. We can make it a holiday for light shining. We can shine light on what it means to be saved, we can spotlight God's goodness (harvest), we can shine a light on saints, we can light a fire, we can spotlight the supernatural, we can shine a light on who we really are, and we can light up the lives of others. And when we do, when we live—and celebrate—as "people who belong to the light," we'll receive "a rich harvest of every kind of goodness, righteousness, and truth" (Ephesians 5:8, 9 GNT).

Veterans Day

"I thank my God every time I remember you"
(Philippians 1:3).

November 11 is a "thank you" holiday. No, I don't have the date wrong. I'm not talking about Thanksgiving, a holiday that comes later this month. I'm talking about Veterans Day, a day to show appreciation to those who have served—or are serving—in the United States military.

November 11 was chosen for this show of appreciation because on this day in 1918 a truce was signed that ended the awful fighting of World War I.[1] This war, which began in 1914, was so terrible and there were so many casualties that a year later, on November 11, 1919, people couldn't help but pause. They were grateful; they wanted to remember those who made peace possible.

This was the beginning of Veterans Day, although it wasn't called that. The day was called Armistice Day (*armistice* means "to stop fighting") because of the truce. It was a day specifically designated to honor World War I veterans, and it might have stayed that way if there hadn't been more wars. Another world war happened and then the Korean War occurred in the early 1950s (1950–53). Congress decided in 1954 that America should honor all war veterans—living and dead. That's when Congress renamed Armistice Day, and November 11 became Veterans Day.

Since 1954, there have been more conflicts keeping the American people conscious of those fighting to preserve our nation's freedom.

Out of this awareness came a desire to also honor those currently serving in the army, the navy, the marines, the air force, and the coast guard as well as those who have served. Realizing that freedom is never free, we now use Veterans Day to respond with gratitude to those who paid—and are paying—freedom's price.

Grateful conversation

Sometimes our awareness—the awareness I mentioned above—needs to be cultivated and nourished, and one way we can do this is by talking.

Talk with your family *about the freedoms* we have. Because military men and women have fought, sacrificed, and worked hard, we are blessed with many freedoms. We have religious freedom. We can choose to pray or not to pray; we can pick where we want to worship and aren't forced to worship in a certain way.

People in the United States can also live where they want in the sense that no one forces them to live in a certain area. Likewise, they have choices about where they work and about whether or not to own a business. They have much latitude to pursue life and happiness. They are free to travel; they aren't restricted by the government. Conversation like this will increase one's appreciation for freedom and for those who make it possible. Members of the armed forces protect us without thinking about the danger to themselves. They fight to protect the rights and freedoms of American citizens.

Talk with young children about *who a veteran is*. What may be so obvious to us may not be to our children. I remember teaching a finger play about Mary and Baby Jesus in a Christmas workshop. An attendee later told me that when he went home, he taught the finger play to his four-year-old daughter. She did the actions about Mary's taking care of Baby Jesus. She seemed to like the finger play, but then she surprised him by asking, "Who is Mary?" The morale of this story is, Never assume!

- Explain that a veteran is someone who *has been* in the armed forces. Many of the veterans we honor are men and women who fought in wars.
- Show pictures of men and women in uniform from magazines or newspapers or from children's books to help them get a picture in their minds.
- Show pictures of anyone in your family, your church, or circle of acquaintances who is serving or has served in the military.

Talk with a veteran. Invite a veteran to dinner and ask him or her to share experiences. Every veteran has stories to tell. Ask the veteran to bring any medals, uniforms, mementos or pictures he or may have and to talk about what he or she did. Ask what it was like to be a soldier, a fighter pilot, or a naval officer. History will come to life right in your own dining room as well as raise your family's consciousness of what Veterans Day is about and why we observe it.

Grateful silence

This seems contradictory to say thank you by keeping silent after suggesting saying thanks by talking. Being silent, though, at a certain time is a traditional way of honoring veterans each November 11.

The armistice occurred at 11:00 in the morning on the 11th day of the 11th month in 1918. Afterward, Australian writer George Honey suggested that people worldwide spend two minutes of silence remembering the soldiers killed in action. Americans liked the idea. It seemed fitting and appropriate, so two minutes of silence became a Veterans Day tradition. People are encouraged to stop and be silent for two minutes to remember those who fought for freedom. In line with the truce, they do this at 11:00 in the morning each November 11.

Where is your family at 11:00? Work? School? If you are homeschooling, then this is something you can indeed choose to do together. On the other hand, you and your family members may be in separate places. If so, talk with them about the day, and ask them if they participated in a moment of silence at 11:00. If they didn't, it's not too late. Pausing to remember is always appropriate, no matter what time it is. The gesture says, "I've got time to remember."

Grateful prayers

When our hearts feel gratitude, as they may through conversation and silent remembering, you may also want to pray out loud.

You might want to have a time of verbal thanks to God as you have your blessing before your evening meal on Veterans Day. This would be a general prayer of thanksgiving for all who have served and are serving. Or you could pray for specific men and women. Have red, white, and blue stars scattered around the table with the names of living veterans or current servicemen and servicewomen written on them. Ask each family member to pick up a star and pray for that person.

You could be more specific in your praying if you invite a veteran to have a meal with you as suggested above. Follow his (or her) sharing of experiences with a prayer of gratitude, thanking God for his courage, his unselfishness, his service, and other specifics you might have gleaned from his sharing.

Likewise, if you visit veterans in hospitals, rehabilitation centers, or nursing homes (as suggested below), hearten their spirits and make them glad they served by praying for them. Thank God for their willingness to serve sacrificially and ask God to bless them and strengthen them.

Grateful greetings

When I asked a veteran in his mid-30s how he preferred being honored on Veterans Day, he said, "The best way I believe to honor veterans is simply to say, 'Thank you.' Taking the time to stop, look them in the eye, and sincerely express your gratitude and respect for them means a great deal. I am glad to see our country, businesses, and organizations take time to honor our veterans with things such as free meals or other special services, but for an individual to take time to thank a veteran seems so much more special. Why? Making it personal seems to make the thanks more meaningful—the words come from someone's heart instead of a being a corporate mandate. It is a sincere expression of gratitude and respect."

In addition to face-to-face words, grateful greetings can also be written. Spend some time together making cards for veterans. These could be cards for veterans you know or for veterans in a hospital or some other institution. On the outside of the cards, family members might draw and color a flag, an eagle, stars, or some other patriotic symbol. They might want to print letters such as *USA* or a big bold *Thank You* on the front. Inside, they can write a thank-you message, like one of these.

- "Thanks for helping to keep America strong and free."
- "Thank you for keeping us safe."
- "Thanks for watching over the USA."
- "I just wanted to let you know how much I appreciate what you've done."

Veterans like getting cards on Veterans Day. The cards show them that people have not forgotten that they fought for the freedom of America. The card says, "We remember what you did, and we are grateful."

Grateful actions

Gratitude doesn't have to always be expressed in messages, cards, words, prayers, silence, or talking. Sometimes gratitude can be expressed by the things we *do*.

Visit veterans in nursing homes, rehabilitation centers, and nursing homes. You may even have a home for veterans in your area. Ask the veterans to talk about their years of service. Give them your undivided attention, allow your face to express interest, your gestures such as the nodding of your head to show understanding, and ask questions that say, "I'm listening, and I want to hear more."

Record a veteran's experiences. Interview a resident in one of the institutions mentioned above or maybe someone in your family or in your church. Make a CD or a DVD of the interview. If you make several copies, he can give them to others. Many older veterans like to know their stories will not be lost. They want to know that future generations will know of their experiences. Be sure to conclude your interview with, "Thank you for sharing."

Invite the family of a deployed serviceman or servicewoman for a meal or do something practical to help them out. If their fall leaves haven't been raked yet, what a great opportunity for you and your family to minister to them.

Help out a disabled veteran or the family of a veteran who has died. Veteran organizations such as the American Legion and the Veterans of Foreign Wars (VFW) can identify needy people for you if you don't know any. These organizations help care for disabled veterans and their families. They also might be able to use your assistance in planning community activities. Organizing and hosting ceremonies is something that these organizations do in addition to looking after veterans and their families.

Wear poppies. In World War I, a soldier by the name of John McCrae wrote a poem called "In Flanders Fields" as a way to remember those who died on the battlefield. He was a doctor who treated many dying men, yet all around him poppies were growing. Such a contrast! Now poppies are a reminder of soldiers who died in combat. When you wear one, you're saying, "I remember, and I'm grateful."

Make a donation. The poppy became the official flower of the VFW. This organization gives the poppies to people. In return, people give money to this veterans group. This money is used to help veterans. Another worthwhile organization to give money to honor veterans is Honor Flight (honorflight.org). The Honor Flight Network is a nonprofit organization that is dedicated to honoring America's veterans for all their sacrifices. As a way of paying tribute to them, they transport veterans to Washington, D.C., where they can visit their war memorials and spend some time reflecting with other veterans. Honor Flight provides these trips for the veterans at no cost to them. A friend of mine who assists in these paid-for trips to war memorials says the veterans are very humble and appreciative. They say things like, "This was the best day of my life"; "Until today I didn't think anyone cared"; and "I'll never forget this day."

Give gifts. Send "We Care" packages to military personnel from your church who are on active duty: toiletries, puzzle books, snacks such as trail mix, and so on. Or take small gifts to residential homes or hospitals for veterans. Contact the institutions first to see what kind of gifts would be appropriate.

Go to a parade. Will Rogers once said, "We can't all be heroes. Some of us have to stand on the curb and clap as they go by." November 11 is when we can clap for our heroes as veteran groups often march in parades in towns, villages, and cities across the country. High school marching bands play music that swells our pride. Patriotism is revealed through floats decorated in red, white, and blue, and military vehicles shine in their glory. Take small flags with you, wave them, and clap as your heroes march by.

Organize a parade. In her book *Veterans Day: Remembering Our War Heroes,* Elaine Landau writes about a community in Pennsylvania that was worried about their Veterans Day parade. The number of veterans in their town was diminishing, but they wanted to keep the parade going. They found a way to do this by asking young people to march along with the veterans.[2] Today many young people march in this parade, keeping a long-standing tradition going, and adding a lively spirit. Let this town's example serve as an inspiration to start a parade in your area. If starting a community-wide parade sounds too daunting, gather the children in your neighborhood. Dress them in red, white, and blue. March down the street singing "Onward, Christian Soldiers."

As you can see, there are many ways to express our appreciation for veterans, for their service, and for their sacrifices. If you want these brave men and women to know how you feel, go to a parade! Wave a flag! Say a prayer! Give them a hand! Say thank you loud and clear.

CHAPTER 18

Thanksgiving

"It is a good thing to give thanks unto the Lord"
(Psalm 92:1 KJV).

The Thanksgiving holiday in the United States hearkens back to what we call "the *first* Thanksgiving." This was when the Pilgrims celebrated surviving their first year in the New World. This wasn't the first-ever Thanksgiving observance, though. Other cultures throughout history including biblical people held thanksgiving celebrations at various times and in various ways. Even other citizens of the New World had times of thanksgiving, and some before the Pilgrims had theirs! It is the experience, though, of the Pilgrims at Plymouth, Massachusetts, that we hold dear and remember each year on the fourth Thursday of November. It is fitting that we should because their story is one of faith, perseverance, and courage.

Inspiring faith

The Plymouth Pilgrims would never have spoken of themselves as Pilgrims. Rather they would say, "We're Separatists." Living in England in the early 1600s, they chose to separate themselves from the state church. They resisted its practices and doctrines. When they refused to conform, they were ridiculed, spied upon, forced to pay fines, and even imprisoned. To escape this persecution, the Separatists went to Holland where they could practice their religion unhindered.

171

The Dutch people were peace-loving and kind. The Separatists could worship as they pleased, but still it wasn't the environment they wanted. They were concerned about bringing up their boys and girls in a manner that was foreign to their own upbringing. Although they had left England, they still wanted their children to be English! And while they were free to worship, they were not allowed to try to make converts. After 12 years and much discussion, they left Holland and headed for the New World.

They started out in two ships, but trouble quickly occurred so they were forced to abandon one ship. Everyone piled onto the *Mayflower*. One hundred and two people crowded into a space about the size of a volleyball court!

Crossing the Atlantic was fraught with danger. The Pilgrims encountered fierce storms and many days of miserable conditions before they arrived at their intended destination of Virginia. It was a cold December day in 1620, and sea conditions were so bad that it made it impossible for them to land. They were forced to sail on to Massachusetts. Once there, their hearts sank again as they surveyed the coastline. It was icy, rocky, and rugged. Beyond the coastline they could see a dense forest. What an unwelcoming, foreboding place! It didn't appear to be conducive to providing a place for a community to develop and to sustain life. Nevertheless, the Pilgrims went ashore and discovered God had a "just right" place waiting for them.

Providence at Plymouth

As they moved onshore and surveyed their surroundings, they found a 20-acre site already cleared, ready for building and planting! The site had four spring-fed creeks nearby to provide their water supply. It sloped gently making it just right for excellent drainage. They knew this was the place to settle, to build their new community!

They worked in earnest to build shelter for themselves. As they worked, they wondered, *What about the winter weather? Will we be able to survive? Who's already here? Are they people to be feared? Or will they be friendly? Will we be able to communicate?*

Their concerns about surviving were legitimate. Many of them had been physically weakened by their long voyage and the demanding work of getting settled. Sickness engulfed them and many died. The colony lost 47 members of the original 102 before spring arrived. Many of the survivors debated whether to return to England, and they might have if it hadn't been for a knock on the door.

In March, as the Pilgrims were discussing defense plans in case of an attack, a visitor appeared at the door of the common house. To their surprise, the visitor was a Native American who wanted to help.

The Native American person was Samoset who could speak some English. He had learned it from a British sea captain who'd made an earlier voyage to Maine. (The Pilgrims were not the first Europeans in this area.) Samoset told them of another Native American, Squanto, who had actually been to England and could speak better English than he could. As it turned out, Squanto was also a Christian. As a young man, he had been kidnapped and taken to England, where he learned English and became a believer.

The governor of the Plymouth colony, William Bradford, said that Squanto, a member of the Patuxet tribe, was sent to them from God. Indeed, it appeared he was. He helped the Pilgrims in many ways. He became their interpreter and helped them make friends with nearby Indian tribes. He also taught them to grow corn, hunt deer, and catch fish. Squanto even taught the Pilgrims how to use fish as a fertilizer to increase the crop yield.

With Squanto's help, the Pilgrims had a harvest by the fall of 1621. Governor Bradford said, "Let's set apart some time for worshipping God and celebrating!" This wasn't the only time of giving thanks that the Pilgrims observed. There would be others. When things happened—or didn't happen!—they paused to give thanks to God. This experience at Plymouth, though, is the one that captures our imagination, lives in our memories, inspires us to count our blessings, and prompts us to express our gratitude to God.

Expressing gratitude

The story of the Pilgrims reminds us to stop and to give thanks. Having a regular day each year designated for this also encourages us, but having a Thanksgiving holiday wasn't something that occurred right away. Times of thanksgiving were celebrated sporadically by the Pilgrims, other New World residents, and in states besides Massachusetts. Many people liked the idea of a designated time of thanksgiving, so, in 1863, President Lincoln made the last Thursday in November a public, legal holiday called Thanksgiving Day. In 1941, Congress changed the date to the fourth Thursday of November. Every year when it rolls around, it's a signal to us: it's time! It's time to pause, to reflect, and to give thanks.

But as much as we like the idea of a Thanksgiving holiday, some of us may be reluctant to actually heed the signal and express our gratitude. The holiday has grown to include more than giving thanks, so we may be tempted to think more about other things. We may focus on the food, football, or shopping. Because it comes around year after year, we may think, *God knows we are thankful*, so we don't actually express our thanks. Some people may even find it awkward to give verbal thanks. Some families solve this by having a designated prayer; he or she always asks the blessing before the Thanksgiving meal. He or she expresses general thanks for everyone. But Thanksgiving will be enhanced—and take on a holy dimension—when we actually express our thanks to God. This doesn't mean we have to do it all the same way or that we shouldn't take into consideration who our guests are and what they would feel comfortable with. There are a variety of ways gratitude may be expressed.

Let others say it for *me.* When your guests arrive, ask them and those who live with you to write what they are thankful for on slips of paper and drop them in a basket. Between the main course and dessert, bring the basket to the dining table. Pass the basket around and ask each person to take one out and read it out loud. Some people are more comfortable reading what others are thankful for than stating what they are thankful for.

"Leaf" me thankful. After the main course while dishes are being cleared and coffee is being prepared, give guests and family members markers and large yellow, brown, and orange paper leaves with strings attached. Ask them to write what they are thankful for on the leaves. Have a Thanksgiving tree nearby (a leafless tree branch set in potting soil). Ask the children to hang the leaves on the tree. As dessert is served, point to the tree and say, "See how thankful we are." Ask the older children to read out loud what is on some of the leaves.

Let others say it with *me outdoors.* Ask family members and/ or friends to take a prayerwalk with you. Walk beside each other, shoulder to shoulder. Designate a place to begin praying and a place to end praying. (Having a designated beginning and end makes everyone more comfortable.) Establish a prayer order—who is going first, who is going next, and so on. At the starting point, the person designated first begins by praying out loud, "Good morning, heavenly Father, on this Thanksgiving Day our group wants to express our gratitude to You. I'll start by thanking You for _____ ." He thanks God for one specific item, and then it is the next person's turn. She thanks God for something, then the next person in the established order, and so on. After each person expresses thanks, it starts over again with the first person as the family continues walking together. If one person finishes, he says, "I pass," when it is his turn. The rest continue to take turns. When your group arrives at the designated ending spot, the first pray-er, the one who began the praying, concludes the group prayer.

Symbolize thanks. About a week before Thanksgiving, place an empty wicker cornucopia, or horn of plenty, in the center of your dining table or on a table in your home that everyone frequently passes by. Ask family members, "What symbol or symbols might characterize your journey and God's provisions in the last year or two? What would represent something for which you are thankful? When you think of a symbol of your thanks, place it in the cornucopia. We'll talk about it and what it means when we have our Thanksgiving meal." Don't have a wicker horn of plenty? Use a regular basket and call it a Bountiful Basket of Blessings. Watch it fill up with specific thanks. On Thanksgiving Day, before—or after—you feast together, lift the basket high—toward heaven and say, "Thanks be to God for His guidance, love, and provisions."

Feather a turkey with thanks. Many pictures of the *first* Thanksgiving include turkeys. Whether they were actually there can't really be proven, but we all believe they were! Turkeys have become a traditional symbol of Thanksgiving, and we can use the image to encourage expressions of gratitude. Make some turkeys *without* feathers out of construction paper. (Think frontal view in the shape of a circle for the body, two feet sticking out at the bottom, and a head with the wattle and the beard at the top.) Also cut out feathers from various colored pieces of construction paper. Have children and guests write what they are thankful for on the feathers. Make sure all the writing is readable. Attach the feathers to the turkeys and display for all to see. As an alternative, make one really large turkey and let each child and guest put *one* thank-you feather on the turkey.

While we don't know for sure if turkeys were a part of the Thanksgiving celebration at Plymouth Rock, we're fairly certain corn and cranberries were. They, too, can be objects for reflection and appreciation.

Native crops

The cranberry is one of three native fruits to North America (blueberries and grapes are the other two), and Native Americans used cranberries in many ways. The Native Americans in northeast America grew three main crops—corn, beans, and squash. Any of these items—the fruits or the vegetables—may be used to encourage thanksgiving. Here are some examples.

Five kernels, five thanks. Squanto, mentioned above, encouraged the Pilgrims to grow corn and to use fish as a fertilizer to increase the crop yield, which they did. And it was a good thing because they would need corn to survive. After the first harvest the Pilgrims experienced and celebrated in the fall of 1621, they had to think about getting through the coming winter. This was a particular concern after more colonists arrived without food, clothing, or supplies. As the Plymouth group surveyed what they had, they realized that their food supply would probably not take them into the next summer. The group, therefore, agreed to ration the corn they had. Each person would get just five kernels per day during the winter of 1621–22. They did this and survived! Consequently, Governor Bradford called for another Thanksgiving celebration in 1622.

Encourage thankfulness by placing five kernels of corn on a fall leaf at each person's plate. The leaf could be a real one that you've gathered and pressed or one made out of construction paper. Tell the story about the daily ration of five kernels of corn for each Pilgrim. Pass a basket around the table and ask each person to name five things he or she is grateful for as he or she places each of the kernels in the basket. To enhance this activity, you might want to read aloud the poem "Five Kernels of Corn" by Hezekiah Butterworth (available online by typing in the author's name and the title of the poem).

Three vegetables, three thanks. Corn, beans, and squash were a prominent part of the diet of Native Americans. They called them the three sisters. Use these vegetables as a centerpiece for your Thanksgiving meal. As you explain this centerpiece, ask those around the table to say three things they are thankful for. This would be a good time to ask them to say three things about the contributions of Native Americans. The survival of the Pilgrims was made possible because of the help they received from those already living here. Of course, the children at your table may enter into this activity more readily if you use the three fruits instead of the three vegetables!

One toast, one prayer. While the cranberry had many uses, one group of Native American Indians used it as a symbol of peace and friendship, and we can too. At each place, have a small glass of cranberry juice. Raise the glasses and drink in honor of Native Americans. Conclude with a prayer of thanks to God for their contributions and a plea for peace and reconciliation. Many people, Native American and non–Native American, hurt over the treatment of Native American Indians. To begin with, the settlers and the Indians lived together peacefully. However, as time passed, the two sides began to fight over land. Wrongs were done, and people were mistreated as the entire continent was taken over by European settlers. At the Thanksgiving holiday, painful memories surface, and we don't have to be insensitive. We can be sensitive—and appreciative—by pausing and lifting our glasses in honor of the first Americans and by praying for reconciliation and healing.

With specific expressions of thanksgiving, our hearts are warmed and we connect with each other and with God. When we do, we experience His presence. He becomes a part of our celebration because God inhabits the praises of His people (Psalm 22:3 KJV).

Expressed thanks, though, isn't the only way to show God our gratitude. Our actions may speak as well. God calls us to practice hospitality (Romans 12:13), and this holiday provides an opportune time for being hospitable.

Being hospitable

The Pilgrims shared their celebration with those who had befriended them. They sent an invitation to Chief Massasoit of the Wampanoag tribe, inviting him and others of the tribe to join their celebration. Chief Massasoit came and brought 90 others with him!

While the Pilgrims hadn't expected so many to respond, they graciously welcomed the Native American Indians, and together, they figured out how to feed the large group. Chief Massasoit quickly assessed the situation and saw they might not have enough food, so he sent some hunters into the woods for more meat. The braves quickly returned with five deer. The resources of the Native American Indians and the Pilgrims were pooled, and the feasting began!

This story gives us a good example of two cultures coming together to work and to play. We can imitate their example at our own Thanksgiving celebration in various ways.

Being hospitable to those who might not be exactly like us. Native Americans helped the Pilgrims through the year so they included them in the feast. When more showed up than they expected, the Pilgrims and the Native Americans worked together to feed everyone. In this spirit, our Thanksgiving feast can be shared with someone of a different culture or background.

- A new immigrant working in your office might be just the person to ask to share in your Thanksgiving feast. Or perhaps he or she has a family and you could invite them all to share your Thanksgiving meal.

- An international student in your community would welcome an invitation to join your family for Thanksgiving dinner. Holidays when many students flee campus can be a very lonely time for students from foreign countries.

- Someone who is culturally different from you who may have been living in your area for some time (no longer an immigrant) but you may have put off getting to know him or her. Perhaps Thanksgiving is the time to get to know this person. Invite him or her to your Thanksgiving feast, and use it as a relationship-building experience.

Ask your invitees to share in the feast as the Native Americans shared in the feast when they were invited by the Pilgrims. Perhaps they could bring a special food item reflective of their country of origin, a story of a thanksgiving custom practiced "back home," a musical number, or a favorite game. All of this will enrich your time together.

Share your emotional and spiritual bounty with those who are needy. Food isn't the only bounty we have to share at Thanksgiving. If we have vital relationships, a home, and a rich faith, we have spiritual and emotional resources to share. We can share these resources by inviting lonely people to eat with us—a lonely widow in your neighborhood whose adult children live far away, a homebound elderly couple who seldom get out and can't cook much for themselves, a young man whose wife died earlier in the year and is finding it hard to think of Thanksgiving without her, or a family having financial problems. This family may have been given a food basket but still feel joyless and discouraged. The warmth of a large gathering may nurture their souls and encourage them.

Share the bounty of your time. Go outside the warmth and comfort of your home to involve your family in some way with people whose lives contrast with yours.

- Help prepare or serve food at a homeless shelter. Be willing to do what is necessary to help with the meal, even going the day before Thanksgiving to assist with the preparation.

- Make something and take to emergency personnel who have to work on Thanksgiving Day. Let them know you are thankful for what they do and the sacrifices they make.

- Spend Thanksgiving afternoon visiting with residents in nursing homes and rehabilitation centers. They may be served a traditional Thanksgiving meal, but feel lonely and forgotten in the afternoon. Your visit can be a day brightener for them.

The thing about sharing your bounty is that it increases your own sense of thankfulness. You may be blessing others, but you will be blessed as you share and interact with others. The contrasts you notice will heighten your awareness of your blessings and you will be moved to express your thanks to God.

Through actions or words—or both—our joy will increase when we express our gratitude. We will understand why the Pilgrims were moved to speak thanks and to invite others to feast with them. More importantly, we will be putting the holy into our holiday.

CHAPTER 19

Christmas

"When they had seen him, they spread the word . . .
and all who heard it were amazed" (Luke 2:17–18).

Christmas is a day and a season. It's a day in the sense that we celebrate Jesus' birthday on December 25, but our observance of His birth begins much earlier. For some, the Christmas season starts the Friday right after Thanksgiving, when the tree goes up. For others, it is the fourth Sunday before Christmas when Advent, a season of spiritual preparation begins. While some start the Christmas season early, others extend it for 12 days afterward. Some do both!

The season encompasses lights, food, parties, gifts, musicals, trees, greeting cards, activities, programs, family times, decorations, and more. We have a myriad of ways of celebrating, and they offer valuable resources and backdrops for celebrating Jesus' birth. No other holiday offers so many possibilities for emphasizing the holy!

The Advent advantage

Long ago, Christians designated the season *before* Christmas Day as a special time. They called it Advent, a word that means "coming," as in Jesus has come, is coming, and will come again. We look back at His birth and life on earth. We know He wants to appear to us in the here and now. And we understand that someday He will come again.

Advent begins on the fourth Sunday before Christmas Day and extends through Christmas Eve, so the number of days of this season can vary from 22 to 28.

As we remember His birth, we get ready for and anticipate Christ's visiting us in the here and now. This is the goal, but ironically Advent occurs when we are easily distracted from thinking about Jesus. The season is crowded and busy with many things vying for our attention and energy. For this reason, families may need some activities to help them be attentive. Two ways we can focus on Jesus during Advent is with a weekly candlelighting ceremony and/or with daily devotional thoughts.

Weekly candlelighting ceremony. A traditional way of recognizing Jesus throughout Advent is with a table wreath that holds four or five candles. You can make your own wreath or purchase one. Starting the fourth Sunday before Christmas, one candle is lit. The next Sunday, two candles are lit. Each week, an additional candle is lit until all the candles are burning. If five candles are used, then the fifth candle is lit on Christmas Eve or Christmas Day.

For this wreath and candles to speak of Jesus, there must be activated symbolism to go along with each candle. Your church may suggest the symbolism along with appropriate prayers, Scriptures, and songs. Here's an outline many including the Poinsett family use.

CANDLE 1: The Promise of Jesus' Coming
BIBLE READING: Isaiah 9:6–7
PRAYER THOUGHT: Prepare our hearts for the celebration of Jesus' birth that we may be filled with wonder and receive Him with praise.
SONG: "O Come, O Come, Emmanuel"

CANDLE 2: Mary and Joseph's Trip to Bethlehem
BIBLE READING: Luke 2:1–5
PRAYER THOUGHT: Just as Mary and Joseph went expectantly to Bethlehem, we expectantly prepare to be ready to receive Jesus.

SONG: "O Come, All Ye Faithful"

CANDLE 3: No Room in the Inn
BIBLE READING: Luke 2:6–7
PRAYER THOUGHT: Jesus, come into our home this Christmas. We have room for You.
SONG: "O Little Town of Bethlehem"

CANDLE 4: The Shepherds Receive the Message from the Angels
BIBLE READING: Luke 2:8–15
PRAYER THOUGHT: Let the glory of the Lord shine upon us and give us peace and gladness. Help us to share our joy with others.
SONG: "Hark! The Herald Angels Sing"

CANDLE 5: The Wise Men Visit the Newborn King
BIBLE READING: Matthew 2:1–2, 9–11
PRAYER THOUGHT: We thank You, God, for the reminder of giving through the gifts of the wisemen. Thank You for the gift of Your Son, Jesus. Thank You for the gifts we receive this Christmas and for the chance to give to others.
SONG: "Joy to the World"

While the Poinsetts use this weekly candlelighting ceremony, we don't use a wreath. We use an inexpensive five-prong candleholder, and it works! It's the doing and the symbolism that helps us focus on Jesus.

Daily devotional activity. Advent calendars are sold this time of year, and they are usually used as a countdown until Christmas as in, "Mom, how many more days until Christmas?" Most of these begin with December 1 and have a 24- or 25-day observance rather than the traditional number of days of Advent. I prefer an activity with a spiritual connection rather than have my family focus on getting gifts.

We use a felt Christmas tree with 25 felt symbols representing the life and nature of Jesus. I wrote 25 devotionals—one to go with each felt symbol—and a friend made the symbols.[1] One symbol is put on a felt tree every day starting December 1. A second is added on December 2, etc. Some of the symbols we use are a Bible, a rose, a manger, a shepherd's crook, a star, the temple, a dove, a goblet, a fish, a boat, a lamp, a door, a lamp, a cross, a butterfly, a crown, etc. All connect with something about Jesus. Each December day through Christmas Day, one family member places a symbol on the tree and another member shares the devotional and explains the symbol's significance.

If the thought of coming up with 25 symbols seems too daunting, then make a paper chain or have your children make one! Each link could contain information about Jesus on one side and the day's number on the other side. A link is subtracted and its contents read each day.

To make a chain of 25 links, you will need 25 strips of paper, about 7½-by-1½ inches. On one side of each strip, write the date (December 1, December 2, etc.). On the other side (what will be the inside of the link), copy a portion of the story of Jesus' birth from an easy-to-read version of the Bible.

If your children are already really familiar with the biblical story of Jesus' birth, you might want to print something else on the inside.

- Bible verses that reflect on what Jesus was like, what He said, and what He did.
- Bible verses that reflect on the *meaning* of Jesus' coming at Bethlehem.
- Bible prophecies that were fulfilled in Jesus' coming.
- Bible verses that refer to Jesus' second coming. As noted above, His *coming* back is a part of the Advent emphasis. We need to be prepared for His coming in the future as well as in the present.

When it's Christmas Eve

The Christmas tree is often more than just another decoration; it is a vibrant part of the spirit of the season. Gather your family and/

or your guests around the tree for Nativity scene activities, singing carols, Scripture reading, or devotional thoughts. But first declare it a nontechie zone.

Determine with your family that Christmas Eve will be a "no screen" time. There won't be any TV, computer, or video game screens. There won't be anyone off in a corner talking on their phones or texting someone. This will be time for reflection, for conversation, for listening to each other, and for listening for Jesus. If we anticipate His coming during Advent, we need to be able to hear Him when He knocks on our heart's door.

- Display your Nativity scene in a ceremonious fashion. My Nativity scenes are up and ready to observe—and play with!—early in the season. One even stays on display all year round! But some families make a special production of bringing out the Nativity scene on Christmas Eve. One family starts the wise men from the far bedroom, replicating their trek from the East to Bethlehem. Another family places all the characters under the tree except Baby Jesus. The next morning, when the children awake, they find Baby Jesus in the manger under the tree.

- Read the biblical account of Jesus birth from either Luke 2 or Matthew 1–2. Or better yet, intertwine the Luke and Matthew accounts. For one continuous story, start with Luke 1:26. When you get to verse 56, go to Matthew 1:18. Read to verse 25, then return to Luke 2:1 and read to verse 38. Finally, turn back to Matthew and read all of chapter 2.

- Share some devotional thoughts. Numerous Christmas stories and devotionals are published in magazines and online each year. What fun it is to read together *The Best Christmas Pageant Ever* by Barbara Robinson! If you haven't read this classic out loud with your family, make it a point to do so, and then talk about the contents. It's a short book, making it possible to cover in one sitting with family members taking turns reading it chapter by chapter. If it seems too long for the ages of your children, start a few nights before Christmas, reading a portion each night.

- Talk about the symbolism of the Christmas tree. According to legend, the Protestant reformer Martin Luther was walking home on a dark December evening when he noticed the starlight coming through the branches of the fir trees near his home. He was so struck and captivated by the beauty that he reproduced the effect in his home. He tied candleholders to an evergreen's branches, put candles in the wooden holders, and lit the candles. He stood back, looked at the effect, and was impressed. To him, the lighted Christmas tree spoke of Jesus. He enhanced on this by teaching "his friends and family that the tree presented the everlasting love of God. He pointed out that the evergreen's color did not fade, just as the Lord's love would not fade, no matter what the circumstance or trial. The candlelight represented the hope that Christ brought to the world through his birth and resurrection."[2]

- Sing carols together. Purchase inexpensive Christmas carol books at discount stores. Bring those out each year for singing or make your own to keep and use year after year. I can hear readers groaning at this suggestion. *Oh no, something complicated to add to an already stressful season.* Start with one page (one song) and inexpensive binders. Add a page every year. I suggest this because singing together is such a spirit-filled holiday activity. To have songbooks ready to use is very helpful. While it may be a little stressful getting these made, you will be thankful in the years following. That's the way I regard the felt wall hanging and symbols our family uses. It's always ready to go every December 1 no matter how busy we may be.

Opening gifts, opening hearts

The focal point for many families at Christmas is the opening of gifts. What are some simple, creative things we can do to add a holy dimension to this activity?

In *Creative Hospitality*, Marlene D. LeFever suggests a candle ceremony to accompany the opening of gifts.[3] After the gifts are opened, the father lights a large candle and places it in the middle of the room. He explains that the large candle is a symbol of Christ, the Light of the world. Then everyone else is given a candle and is invited to take his unlit candle to the large one and light it. In this way he is saying that he wants Christ to shine through his life. After the candles are burning, the family might sing the doxology or "I Have Decided to Follow Jesus." This simple ceremony takes only a few minutes, and yet it is says so much at a time when Jesus may be overlooked.

One family I read about draws closer to Christ by praying for each other after they open their gifts. With paper and bows still scattered around the family room, a parent asks each family member to answer this question: "If I could ask God to do just one thing in my life or in the life of my family over the next year, what would that one thing be?" No one is allowed to critique, challenge, or give advice to another family member when he or she answers the question. Rather it is a time to listen and then to pray. The individual who answered moves to the center of the room. The entire group gathers around, lays hands on the person, and prays for him or her. Tears are shed and relationships deepened as God responds with affirmation and love.

Another family prepares golden gift boxes to give golden words to each other. They collect small boxes like earring boxes or matchboxes and print Bible verses to go inside. They draw names so everyone is preparing a box and everyone will receive one. The verse could be a blessing such as, "The Lord bless you and keep you, the Lord make his face shine upon you and be gracious to you; the Lord turn his face toward you and give you peace" (Numbers 6:24–26). It could be a reminder of Jesus' presence: "Never will I leave you; never will I forsake you" (Hebrews 13:5). Or it could be something declarative about Jesus' nature: "I am the resurrection and the life" (John 11:25).

The boxes are then wrapped in gold paper and placed under the tree. When the other gifts are opened, the family members can open their "treasures."

Making Christ the centerpiece

Many of us like to open our homes at Christmas for large gatherings, dinners, or parties during the Christmas season. Even in these events, our focus can be on honoring Jesus by making Him the centerpiece. At the table, it can be some prepared questions to answer, a thought-provoking object, a responsive reading, or an activity between the main course and dessert. At a large gathering where we're not seated at a table, make Jesus the centerpiece of the gathering. A good time to make Him the focus is after several games have been played but before refreshments are served.

A birthday cake. If your festive event includes several children, make Jesus the centerpiece by having a birthday cake for Him. Children understand birthday cakes, making it a good symbol to connect them with Jesus. There are a variety of ways the cake can be decorated, even in a symbolic way. Here's one family's symbolism.

- The cake is white with white icing to represent purity.
- The bottom layer is round to picture the world.
- The second layer is star-shaped, recalling the star of Bethlehem.
- An angel sits atop the star as a reminder that an angel announced Jesus' birth to Mary and to the shepherds.
- The first layer has 20 green candles—one for each century since the first Christmas and green to represent the ever-living Christ.
- The lighted candles represent Jesus' being the Light of the world.

While I appreciate the symbolism of this family's cake, I could never pull off a star-shaped second layer! Two round layers of white cake with white icing and a miniature manger scene on top would work at our house. Either way, children will appreciate and understand the symbolism. When you are ready for refreshments, gather everyone around the cake, sing "Happy Birthday" to Jesus, and blow out the candles.

Stories told well—or even read well—provide a simple and effective way for turning thoughts toward Jesus. Stories capture attention, touch emotions, and move spirits. They can provide a good spiritual emphasis to round out or end a party. Be on the lookout in late November and December for good Christmas material to share. I've found articles in *Guideposts, Reader's Digest,* and even the *Wall Street Journal.* Numerous books such as *The Spirit of Christmas* offer compilations of stories where you will be able to find one that suits your event and your guests. *The Tale of Three Trees,* a book that retells a very old story, makes a good centerpiece because it links Jesus's birth with the Cross.

Sharing of meaningful experiences. This could be someone's personal testimony about God's gift of love to them or about how they became acquainted with Jesus. Or you could have several individuals tell about meaningful personal or family stories from Christmases past that reflect Christ. Many times in my parents' home our faith was strengthened when our parents told about how God blessed them through a grocer's kind act during World War II when their Christmas was going to be bleak.[4]

These are all ways you can focus on Jesus, have a good time, and minister to others when you have people *coming* to your home. Christmas is also about *going*—going to where people are and telling the story.

"Go, 'Yell' It on the Mountain"

At a Merry Missions Christmas program, my husband talked about the shepherds and wise men being "let's *go*" type of people. They got up and left their responsibilities and went to another place. He then linked them to missionaries who are "let's *go*" type of people.

Another man led in a prayer for international missionaries, for they are certainly "let's *go*" people.

Communicating the gospel is also a challenge for missionaries in North America so I told a story from Donna Thomas's book *Faces in the Crowd*. A Jordanian student she was working with asked, "Is Santa Claus Jesus' father?" Internationals like this student may be wondering at some of the things we do at Christmas. Getting to know them so they feel comfortable enough to ask is an important part of a missionary's work. One of the women in the group led in a prayer for North American missionaries. Then I said, "We have the same challenge and we need to go to others and tell Jesus' story. Christmas gives us an opportune time for doing this."

Naturally, after all this talk about *going*, we concluded with singing "Go, Tell It on the Mountain." Then a gentleman suggested we need to yell out the good news so we did. We loudly cheered: "Jesus Christ is born!" I would like to think it was the moving program that led him to make this suggestion, but maybe the idea had been planted in his head the previous Sunday morning. A mistake had been made in the church bulletin. The printed title of a song we were to sing was "Go, Yell It on the Mountain." How appropriate! We have "good news of great joy . . . for all the people . . . a Savior has been born" (Luke 2:10–11). This is news to share!

Go, tell families. I think there are families, even those who don't go to church, who would like to honor Jesus at Christmas, but they don't know how to do something that would be kid-friendly. You can help.

- Purchase inexpensive, punch-out cardboard Nativity scenes or storybooks about Jesus' birth to include in food baskets that your church prepares for and delivers to hard-pressed families.
- Prepare an Advent observance like the chain mentioned above or the felt tree with its 25 felt symbols. One woman I know made the felt symbols, the felt tree, printed the devotionals, and delivered them to families in a low-income housing area near her church. A women's group prepared these for all the children who rode

the bus to participate in their church's Wednesday night outreach program.

- A teenager made the paper chains with verses printed inside and gave them to the families where she was the babysitter.

Go, tell elderly mothers and fathers. Janet Erwin, editor of *Missions Mosaic* magazine, told me about her mother's first Christmas in an assisted-living residence. She wrote,

"We drove almost two hours on Christmas Day to see her and got there at 2:00 in the afternoon. My older son plays the guitar and he and my husband sing so I had asked the director if we could do a little 'program' for the residents who couldn't get away with family or had no one coming to see them. The director agreed, so at 4:30, Trey and Monte led us in Christmas carols while Trent (my younger son) interspersed the songs with portions of the Bible story from *The Message*. (Both sons are college students.) Monte shared with them the story behind 'Silent Night' and Trey (who has been studying German for four years and was a summer missionary there last summer) sang the song in German. Then I shared with them the book *The Legend of the Candy Cane*. I had packaged materials for them to make candy canes out of pipe cleaners and beads. We helped those who couldn't see well or whose hands were too arthritic to work well. I gave them real candy canes as a treat. We were graciously received. On the way, my sons had said, 'We don't know how to work with older people.' I had assured them it was a lot like working with children. When we got in the car to return home, Trey said, 'You're right, Mom. It is like with working with children, but with children who have manners.' The residents were very grateful someone brought them a Christmas experience that focused on Jesus."

Go, see the bereaved. Purchase little picture frame Christmas tree ornaments at a craft store. Personally deliver these in early December to those in your church family or of your acquaintance who lost a loved one during the past year. Encourage the recipient to put a picture of the deceased in the frame and place it on their tree in his or her memory. This simple gesture means so much to the bereaved. It reminds them that someone cares and is sensitive to their keen feelings of loss as the holiday approaches. It also provides them with a way to include their loved one in their Christmas observance.

Go, and sing. Christmas caroling is an old custom, but one that can still be meaningful and effective. Get a group together and seek permission to carol in the halls of hospitals, rehab centers, and nursing homes. If you've ever been hospitalized at Christmas, as I have been, you know how much cheer caroling can bring to patients, especially if carolers smile a lot, greet the patients, and shake hands where possible.

Go, and say, "Come." Music is an important part of Christmas, and people look for concert events at Christmas. Many people from the community who would never attend a regular church service are often receptive to attending a musical program, so invite unbelievers to church cantatas and musical programs. Invite a family who has just moved to your area or just joined your church to share in your Christmas festivities.

This list could go on and on, because once we catch the spirit of Jesus, the importance of His coming—in the past, in the present, and in the future—we have good news to share. We have something to yell about! Don't you agree?

Kwanzaa

"Celebrate the Feast of the Harvest
. . . Bring the best of the firstfruits of
your soil to the house of the Lord your God"
(Exodus 23:16, 19).

*K*wanzaa is an end-of-the-year holiday that's well suited for an end-of-the-book chapter, and here's why. It makes use of various celebration tools this book has proposed using—stories, symbols, candles, food, gifts, displays, questions, history, values, and conversation. If there is a holiday you want to celebrate—one that isn't mentioned in this book—and you want to put the holy into it, you can draw on these tools.

This is not to say that Kwanzaa is like other holidays. It isn't. For one thing, it is not a day. It is a festival that begins on December 26 and ends on January 1.

For another thing, it is devoted to recognizing and appreciating African American culture and history. Irish celebrate their heritage on St. Patrick's Day, even though the day began as a remembrance of St. Patrick. Italians use Columbus Day to emphasize theirs, although the holiday originally commemorated the discovery of America. Mexican Americans celebrate their heritage on Cinco de Mayo, a holiday that recalls a famous battle. Kwanzaa, though, isn't an add-on to something else. Its specific purpose is to recognize and strengthen the African American community.

Seven points of strength

In 1966, Dr. Maulana Karenga, a California State University professor of black studies, wanted African Americans to build strong families and communities. He believed having their own holiday would be a way to do this. He wrote seven principles for African Americans to celebrate and to live by.

Unity. Instead of living separate lives, African Americans are to live and work together in harmony.

Self-determination. Instead of letting someone else make decisions, African Americans are to make their own choices about who they want to be and what they want to do.

Collective work and responsibility. Living successfully in a community means helping each other and solving problems together.

Cooperative economics. Community means not only living together in harmony, but it also means using your financial resources to help others so all will profit.

Purpose. A stronger community is built if goals are set and reached, when people live in a way that is useful to others.

Creativity. A community can be improved and beautified with new ways and new ideas.

Faith. Individuals are to believe in themselves, in others, particularly leaders, and in having a bright future.

These are good principles to hold on to and to practice. You will note, though, that none of them mention God, not even the faith principle. Nowhere are people encouraged to give thanks to God or even to recognize God. This is one reason why some believers question whether or not to observe Kwanzaa.

To Kwanzaa or not Kwanzaa

Perhaps the biggest resistance to observing Kwanzaa goes back to its formation. In the beginning, Dr. Karenga said that Kwanzaa was to be an alternative to Christmas. He said that Christianity was a white religion which black people should shun and that Jesus was psychotic.

However, as time passed, Kwanzaa gained some mainstream support. There were African American Christians who wanted to celebrate their heritage. The holiday reminded them: Stop and pay attention to who you are and where you came from. Noticing this, Dr. Karenga altered his position. In 1997, he described Kwanzaa as a supplement to Christmas and not an alternative.

Consequently, some African American Christians observe Kwanzaa and even regard its guiding principles as Christian principles. Some churches display Kwanzaa's symbolic candleholder and candles along with the Advent wreath and its candles. They include appropriate prayers and readings into their worship services.

The purpose of this chapter is not to convince you either way. The purpose is to help you understand Kwanzaa, what it is about, and how it is celebrated; and if you choose to celebrate it, a few ideas on putting the holy into this holiday.

Keep seven in mind!

Kwanzaa features *seven* principles over s*even* days using *seven candles* and s*even* symbols. The seven symbols include a unity cup, a candleholder, seven candles, a woven mat, gifts, corn, and crops. Each item has a special meaning.

Unity cup. This is a special cup that everyone drinks from each day of the celebration. As they do, they say, "Let's all pull together."

The candleholder. The candleholder stands for people who lived long ago in Africa. In other words, Africans hold up African Americans just as the candleholder holds candles.

Seven candles. Each candle stands for one of the seven principles, and each candle's color also has meaning. A black candle is in the center of the candleholder, three red ones are on the left, and three green ones are on the right. Black stands for African Americans and all people of Africa. Red stands for their struggles. Green stands for hope and the future.

A woven mat or straw mat is a symbol of history. Other symbols are placed on the mat as a way of saying, "Today stands on yesterday."

Corn. The corn stands for children, so one ear of corn is placed on the mat for each child. If there are no children, two ears of corn are put on the mat.

Gifts. Presents are given to the children. The gifts stand for rewards for keeping the principles during the past year.

Crops. A basket of fruit and vegetables is set on the mat. The crops stand for hard work and the harvest. It is this concept of harvest that gives Kwanzaa its name.

Kwanzaa's name comes from the Swahili language of Africa. Kwanzaa means "firstfruits" of the harvest. Christians are familiar with this term as it appears frequently the Bible. *Firstfruits* was originally associated with the harvests of barley and wheat, but eventually it came to mean giving our first and our best to God. Kwanzaa, though, does not recognize God as the source of the harvest or encourage expression of gratitude to Him. This is one place where we can add a holy dimension. We can "bring the best of the firstfruits of" our "soil" and offer them to God (see Exodus 23:19).

Gather the symbols and display them. Most of the Kwanzaa symbols are placed on a table for all to see, starting with the mat. The other symbols are arranged on the mat so people can look at the display and tell what Kwanzaa is about during the seven-day celebration. Ask your family what Christian symbol or symbols you could add to the scene. What could you add to the scene that would make it say to others, "Here is a Christian celebration of African American heritage"? What could you add that would say to God, "I acknowledge Your blessing us with a harvest"?

Make a ceremony out of displaying the symbols. Have children coming from different areas of the house carrying the candleholder, the candles, and the unity cup. After the children have marched and the items are arranged, join hands for a prayer of thanks for all the symbols and what they stand for.

Wave the corn before God. Sound crazy? Actually this is what God's people did many years ago when observing a harvest festival. In presenting the firstfruits, they took a sheaf of barley or a sheaf of wheat and waved the sheaves before God.[1] Each child can pick up his ear of corn, walk back and forth to the north, the south, the east, and the west waving it before God.

Make a second or third table display. In addition to having a display of the Kwanzaa symbols, have a second one duplicating the story of God's people escaping slavery and heading toward the Promised Land. What symbols would you use to represent their leaving Egypt? Would you have a red tablecloth for the parting of the Red Sea? The number 10 for their guiding principles, the Ten Commandments? You would definitely want milk and honey on the table to represent the Promised Land. A third table display could represent Christians. Would you start with the Cross or the manger? Would you use a fish for fishers of men? How would you represent the church that Jesus built? A rock, a building, a group of people? What would be your symbol for the coming of the Holy Spirit? Would you have candles as a part of the display?

Celebrating with candles

It's interesting to me that Christmas, Hanukkah (a December Jewish festival), and Kwanzaa all use candles for celebrating. During the Christmas season, Christians honor the Light of the world with symbolic Advent candles. Hanukkah relates back to the Jews' gaining religious freedom after their oppressors desecrated the temple and tried to force them to worship Zeus. When the Jews cleaned up the temple, they rekindled the flame of the Eternal Light. Only one day's worth of oil could be found, yet it took eight days until fresh oil could be brought into the temple. Miraculously, the single day's supply burned for eight days and eight nights. Jews celebrate Hanukkah to remember this miracle, lighting a new candle each night of this eight-day festival.

In a similar way, those celebrating Kwanzaa light candles every day. In addition, everyone discusses the principle for that day and drinks from the unity cup. There's a prescribed order in the lighting.

- *Day one:* The black candle (the middle candle) is lit, and unity is discussed.
- *Day two:* the family relights the black candle, lights the first red candle, and talks about self-determination.
- *Day three:* The family relights the black and red candles, and lights the first green candle as they pledge to work together.
- *Day four:* Celebrants relight the candles for the first three days, as well as another red candle. They converse about cooperative economics.
- *Day five:* Participants light the candles from the first four days, as well as another green candle. They ponder their usefulness to the African American community.
- *Day six:* The first five candles are relit and the third red candle is lit. In addition, they may express their creativity by telling stories, playing African American instruments, or making up songs.
- *Day seven:* All the previous six candles are relit, and the final green candle is lit. Celebrants reflect on the faith they have in themselves, in their family, in their leaders, and in their African heritage.

How can we add a holy dimension to an activity that is already filled with meaning and symbolism? We can do it in three ways.

1. *Voice a prayer* each day to accompany the lighting of the new candle or to follow the discussion of the featured principle. For example, for the first day, when you light the unity candle, you might pray something like this: "Father, as we display our heritage, as we think about ourselves as a people, help us to work together to

strengthen our families and our communities. Help us to not be so concerned about our own doings, but get a bigger picture and think about our community as a whole. Help us to work together for a brighter future."

Another prayer option is to say the Lord's Prayer together as you light the candles. The Lord's Prayer is a community prayer: "*Our* Father"; "Give *us* this day"; "Lead *us* not into temptation"; etc. This prayer is most appropriate for a group that wants to work together and strengthen community.

2. *Read a Bible passage* each day that offers a scriptural basis or support for each candle's emphasis. Use a clear, easy-to-listen-to version of the Bible. Here's a suggestion for each day.

- Unity—Ephesians 4:1–6
- Self-determination—Philippians 3:12–17
- Collective work and responsibility—1 Thessalonians 5:12–14 or 2 Thessalonians 3:6–10
- Cooperative economics—2 Corinthians 9:10–15
- Purpose—Hebrews 13:1–7
- Creativity—1 Corinthians 12:4–11
- Faith—Ephesians 1:15–23

3. *Pick a Christian song to sing* each day of Kwanzaa.

- Unity: "We Are One in the Spirit"
- Self-determination: "I Have Decided to Follow Jesus"
- Collective work and responsibility: "Work for the Night Is Coming"
- Cooperative economics: "Make Me a Blessing"
- Purpose: "Something for Thee"
- Creativity: "How Great Thou Art"
- Faith: "Faith Is the Victory"

Work together to make their Kwanzaa "playlist." That would certainly entail putting the collective work principle into practice!

Bringing the community together

The sixth day of Kwanzaa is feast day! It's also New Year's Eve when many people are celebrating, so this is a great opportunity to bring family, friends, acquaintances, and even strangers together for food and fellowship.

If you're African American, you can promote understanding by inviting African Americans you don't know well to share your feast with you. Look particularly for those families who need encouragement or who are having a hard time financially to share the feast's bounty.

Or invite those who aren't African American so you can share your culture, your music, and your history with them. Use this feast as an opportunity to educate others.

If you're not African American, you might want to host a feast on New Year's Eve and make sure you invite African Americans. Ask them to share at your gathering what Kwanzaa is all about.

In either case, insist that your guests bring something to contribute to the meal. This involves practicing the collective work and economic cooperation principles!

Celebrate with music using African songs and their traditional musical instruments.

Tells stories that reveal and reinforce African American heritage.

- The stories could be of well-known African Americans such as Martin Luther King Jr., Rosa Parks, Jackie Robinson, Harriet Tubman, Colin Powell, and George Washington Carver.
- The stories could be of your ancestors. Every family has remarkable men and women in their family's past, people who never made the history books, but who contributed to who we are and whose stories inspire us.
- The stories could be about Africans in the Bible: Nimrod (Genesis 10:6–12); Zipporah (Moses' wife, Exodus 2:21–22; 4:24–26; 18:1–6; Numbers 12:1); the Queen of Sheba (1 Kings 10:1–13;

2 Chronicles 9:1–12); Simon of Cyrene (Matthew 27:32; Mark 15:21; Luke 23:26); and the Ethiopian eunuch (Acts 8:26–40). Of course, you might want to skip this last person if you're uncomfortable about explaining to your children what a eunuch is! On the other hand, it is a great story of spiritual transformation.

Finish the feast by talking about the New Year. During Kwanzaa, people not only look back, they also look forward. Ask participants what blessings they anticipate experiencing in the New Year. Conclude the sharing with repeating together Jabez's prayer: "Oh, that you would bless me and enlarge my territory! Let your hand be with me, and keep me from harm so that I will be free from pain" (1 Chronicles 4:10).

While Kwanzaa is a relatively new holiday compared with many of the holidays in this book, it uses tried-and-true celebration tools: candles, symbols, displays, prayers, songs, readings, feasting, etc. I hope this encourages you to feel confident about celebrating any holiday. There are many more besides the 19 in this book, and who knows? Maybe someone else will come along like Dr. Karenga and see something that needs to be celebrated. Maybe that person will be *you*; and if it is, you can say, "I can do that. I know how to put the holy into holidays."

Endnotes

CHAPTER 2

[1]There are exceptions. For instance, Jews celebrate Rosh Hashanah sometime in September or October. Chinese celebrate the New Year for two consecutive weeks usually starting in late January or early February.

[2]Page Hughes, *Party with a Purpose* (Birmingham, AL: New Hope Publishers, 2003), 80.

[3]Bernadette McCarver Snyder, *Saintly Celebrations & Holy Holidays* (Liguori, MO: Liguori, 1997, 12.

[4]Ibid.

[5]Michele Guinness, *The Heavenly Party* (Grand Rapids, MI: Monarch Books, 2007), 115.

CHAPTER 3

[1]Cindy Salzmann, *Beyond Groundhogs and Gobblers: Putting Meaning Back into Your Holiday Celebrations* (Camp Hill, PA: Christian Publications, Inc., 2004), 14.

[2]Reagan Miller, *Martin Luther King, Jr. Day* (New York: Crabtree Publishing, Company, 2009), 26.

CHAPTER 4

[1]Ann Heinrichs, *Valentine's Day* (Chanhassen, MN: The Child's World, 2006), 8.

[2]Ibid., 25.

[3]Joyce Rogers, "Share the Love," *Guideposts*, February 2012, 8.

CHAPTER 5

[1]C. W. Bess, *Object-Centered Children's Sermons* (Grand Rapids, MI: Baker Book House, 1978), 107–8.

[2]Bernadette McCarver Snyder, *Saintly Celebrations & Holy Holidays* (Liguori, MO: Liguori, 1997), 21.

[3]Cyndy Salzmann, *Beyond Groundhogs and Gobblers: Putting Meaning Back into Your Holiday Celebrations* (Camp Hill, PA: Christian Publications Inc., 2004), 28.

[4]Gordon Leidner, "Lincoln's Faith in God," Great American History, http://www.greatamericanhistory.net/lincolnsfaith.htm (accessed February 13, 2012).

[5]Rebecca Price Janney, *Who Goes There?* (Chicago: Moody Publishers, 2009), 51.

CHAPTER 6

[1]Leon McBeth, *Men Who Made Missions* (Nashville: Broadman Press, 1968), 16.

[2]Ibid., 17.

[3]Ibid., 18.

[4]St. Patrick's Day commemorates the anniversary of his death which was probably in A.D. 461, but that year is not absolute.

[5]Answers to quiz: (1) Joseph; (2) Moses; (3) Paul; (4) Paul; (5) Elijah; (6) Paul; (7) Paul.

CHAPTER 7

[1]A complete list of the symbols we used, an explanation of their symbolism, and corresponding Scriptures are found in author's book *Celebrations That Touch the Heart* and on her Web site (BrendaPoinsett.com).

CHAPTER 8

[1]Carol Gnojewski, *Cinco de Mayo: Celebrating Hispanic Pride* (Berkeley Heights, NJ: 2002), 17–18.

[2]Janice Levy, *Celebrate! It's Cinco De Mayo!* (Morton Grove, IL: Albert Whitman and Company, 2007), last page in book. (The book's pages aren't numbered.)

[3]Also known as "Trading My Sorrows."

[4]Exodus 3:8; 3:17; 13:5; 33:3; Leviticus 20:24; Numbers 13:27; 14:8; Deuteronomy 26:9,15; 27:3.

CHAPTER 9

[1]Answers: (1) C; (2) G; (3) A; (4) H; (5) J; (6) E; (7) F; (8) I; (9) B; (10) D.

[2]Answers: (1) Eve (Genesis 3:20); (2) Timothy's mother, Eunice (2 Timothy 1:5); (3) Rebekah (Genesis 27:5–13); (4) Hannah (1 Samuel 1:10–11, 28); (5) Hagar (Genesis 21:1–10, 14); (6) Zebedee's wife, the mother of James and John (Matthew 20:20–21); (7) John (John 19:27); (8) the widow of Nain (Luke 7:12–15); (9) Peter's wife's mother (Matthew 8:14–15); (10) Herodias (Matthew 14:6–8).

CHAPTER 10

[1]Dian Thomas, *Holiday Fun Year-Round* (Holladay, UT: The Dian Thomas Company, 1995), 73.

[2]Ibid.

CHAPTER 11

[1]Some sources discount Betsy Ross's having made the first flag.

[2]Unlike the pledge to the American flag, there is not one standard pledge to the Christian flag. The one I've included here is a common one, but yours may differ. This could be a topic of discussion: What should really be said in the pledge to the Christian flag? Does it represent what I believe?

[3]Paul W. Powell, *Special Sermons for Special Days* (Dallas: Annuity Board of the Southern Baptist Convention, 1993), 39.

[4]From second verse of "The Star-Spangled Banner."

CHAPTER 12

[1]Answers: (1) Adam (Genesis 4:1–2, 25); (2) Noah (Genesis 6:10; 7:7); (3) Abraham (Genesis 22:3); (4) Isaac (Genesis 27:14–29); (5) Jacob (Genesis 37:17–28); (6) Saul

(1 Samuel 19:1–2; 9–11); (7) David (2 Samuel 18:33); (8) Laban (Genesis 29:16); (9) Jairus (Mark 5:22–23, 40–42); (10) Zechariah (Luke 1:20).

[2]Dian Thomas, *Holiday Fun Year-Round* (Holladay, UT: The Dian Thomas Company, 1995), 84.

[3]Ibid.

[4]Ibid.

[5]A red rose means the father is living. A white rose means he has died but your love for him continues to live.

CHAPTER 13

[1]Peter Marshall and David Manuel, *The Light and the Glory* (Old Tappan, NJ: Fleming H. Revell Company, 1977), 310–11.

[2]Ibid., 310.

[3]Ibid., 311.

CHAPTER 14

[1]This is an old but lively hymn, just right for marching. If you don't know this hymn, then use the words as chant, with the children heavily stepping along.

CHAPTER 16

[1]Richard J. Foster, *Celebration of Discipline* (New York,: Harper & Row, Publishers, Inc., 1978, 170.

CHAPTER 17

[1]The armistice was a cease fire, a stopping of the fighting. World War I officially ended with the signing of the Treaty of Versailles in June 1919.

[2]Elaine Landau, *Veterans Day: Remembering Our War Heroes* (Berkeley Heights, NJ: Enslow Publishers, Inc., 2002), 25.

CHAPTER 19

[1]The complete devotionals plus the symbols and instructions for making a felt tree wall hanging are available in author's booklet "Miracle on 25th Street," available through her Web site (BrendaPoinsett.com).

[2]Ace Collins, *Stories Behind the Great Traditions of Christmas* (Grand Rapids, MI: Zondervan, 2003), 73–74.

[3]Marlene D. LeFever, *Creative Hospitality* (Wheaton, IL: Tyndale House Publishers, 1980), 169.

[4]A brief version of this story appears on pages 124–25 in author's book *Can Martha Have a Mary Christmas?*

CHAPTER 20

[1]They could also remove the grain from the sheaves, make bread, and wave the bread before the Lord.

Christmas Books by Brenda

Can Martha Have a Mary Christmas?
Untangling Expectations and Truly Experiencing Jesus
ISBN-13: 978-1-56309-931-1
N054117 • $9.99

Unwrapping Martha's Joy
Creating a Mary Christmas in Your Heart and Home
ISBN-13: 978-1-59669-327-2
N124134 • $14.99

Available in bookstores everywhere

For information about these books or authors, visit NewHopeDigital.com

New Hope® Publishers is a division of WMU®, an international organization that challenges Christian believers to understand and be radically involved in God's mission. For more information about WMU, go to wmu.com. More information about New Hope books may be found at NewHopeDigital.com. New Hope books may be purchased at your local bookstore.

Use the QR reader on your
smartphone to visit us online at
NewHopeDigital.com

If you've been blessed by this book, we would like to hear your story. The publisher and author welcome your comments and suggestions at: newhopereader@wmu.org.